RETHINKING
CONSTITUTIONAL
LAW

RETHINKING CONSTITUTIONAL LAW

ORIGINALISM, INTERVENTIONISM, AND THE POLITICS OF JUDICIAL REVIEW

Earl M. Maltz

 University Press of Kansas

© 1994 by the University Press of Kansas

Published by the University Press of Kansas (Lawrence, Kansas 66049), which was organized by the Kansas Board of Regents and is operated and funded by Emporia State University, Fort Hays State University, Kansas State University, Pittsburg State University, the University of Kansas, and Wichita State University

Library of Congress Cataloging-in-Publication Data

Maltz, Earl M., 1950–
    Rethinking constitutional law : originalism, interventionism and
the politics of judicial review / Earl M. Maltz.
      p.   cm.
    Includes bibliographical references and index.
    ISBN 0-7006-0653-X (hardcover : acid free paper)
    1. United States—Constitutional law—Interpretation and
construction.   2. Judicial review—United States.   3. Law and
politics.   I. Title.
    KF4550.M26   1993
    342.73—dc20
    [347.302]   93-30266

British Library Cataloguing in Publication Data is available.

Printed in the United States of America
10 9 8 7 6 5 4 3 2 1

The paper used in this publication meets the minimum requirements of the American National Standard for Permanence of Paper for Printed Library Materials Z39.48-1984.

CONTENTS

PREFACE

The debate over constitutional theory is as old as the republic itself. The participants in the debate have been divided along a number of different lines. On the most simplistic level, the division is purely political. The Supreme Court is a repository of considerable political power, and its most controversial constitutional decisions are often analyzed in terms of their impact on the balance of power between liberal and conservative political forces.

The second major theoretical divide focuses on the frequency with which the Constitution is invoked as the basis for decision in cases that come before the Court. Interventionists argue that the Court should frequently invoke the Constitution to displace the results that would be reached by the Court in the absence of constitutional constraints. Noninterventionists, by contrast, argue that the Constitution should play only a minor role in judicial decisionmaking. Noninterventionists are often described as supporting judicial deference.

Finally, the division between originalists and nonoriginalists has been one of the most persistent features of the debate. Originalists hold that the Court should interpret the Constitution to reflect the original understanding of the framers, while nonoriginalists believe that some other approach is more appropriate. Although originalism is currently out of fashion with academics, it claims the allegiance of a number of the justices currently sitting on the Court.

In the contemporary debate over constitutional theory, the interaction between these various categories has become distorted. Until quite recently, most theorists (and virtually all of the popular press) have associated deference with political conservatism and interventionism with the forces of liberalism and the more extreme left. Moreover, supporters of originalism have generally characterized themselves (and been characterized by nonoriginalists) as being opposed to interventionism. Thus, the universe of constitutional theory is seen as divided between two viewpoints: conservative/originalist/noninterventionist and leftist/nonoriginalist/interventionist.

This bipolar view of the world was reflected in the scholarly criticism of the Court's recent decisions in *Wygant v. Jackson Board of Education*[1] and *City of Richmond v. J. A. Croson Co.*[2] In both these cases, the Court overturned voluntarily adopted, race-conscious affirmative action programs. Some of the criticism overtly challenges the substantive vision of racial equality underlying *Wygant* and *Croson*.[3] Commentators such as David Chang, by contrast, take the justices to task for abandoning their professed "judicial conservatism."[4] Chang argues that "the essence of judicial conservatism is a reluctance to make choices among controversial competing policies . . . without clear guidance from a constitutionally-rooted hierarchy of values"[5] and that "judicial conservatives are concerned about *both* enforcing firmly established constitutional values *and* not erroneously intruding on valid democratic discretion."[6]

Of course, there is nothing untoward about arguing against judicial interventionism. However, any attempt to link conservatism, originalism, and noninterventionism necessarily distorts the debate over constitutional theory. Analytically, there is no reason why one cannot be a liberal originalist or a conservative interventionist. Indeed, as we will see, virtually the only two labels that *cannot* fit together are originalist and noninterventionist. By linking these disparate concepts, the bulk of the current literature confuses the analysis of both originalism and interventionism.

In this study I take a somewhat different tack. I begin by discussing the political context that has both shaped and marred the debate over constitutional interpretation. Next, rather than comparing originalist analysis to nonoriginalist interventionism, and various noninterventionist approaches to one another, I compare all these approaches to what might be described as a constitutional state of nature—a regime under which the written constitution would play no role in judicial decisionmaking. I hope that this approach will cast new light on the issues that divide constitutional theorists.

While the focus of the book is constitutional theory, it is also in some respects a work of constitutional history as well. By this I do not mean to claim to be providing major new insights into the ideas that have influenced American constitutional development. However, a relatively detailed historical discussion of the evolution of some aspects of American constitutional law is necessary to avoid defects that have infected much of the existing literature.

First, any plausible discussion of constitutional theory generally must be firmly rooted in knowledge of the original understanding itself. While pure originalism is in some disrepute, most competing theories attempt somehow to connect their arguments to the original understanding. Unfortunately, the historical analysis that underlies these claims is sometimes shockingly thin. Some commentators look at the language of the Constitution (particularly the Fourteenth Amendment) and make unsupported assumptions about what the framers "must" have meant; others base their arguments on vastly oversimplified theories regarding the historical background of the original understanding. I have attempted to avoid these problems by drawing on the work of distinguished historians for an understanding of the founding period and on my own research into primary sources for the background of the Reconstruction amendments.[7]

The other major historical element involved in studies of constitutional theory is more straightforward. Most approaches to constitutional analysis are based either implicitly or explicitly on predictions of the results that judges would reach if they adopted a particular mode of analysis. These predictions must be measured against the record of the actual behavior of the Supreme Court. Many commentators focus nearly all their attention on decisions rendered in the second half of the twentieth century. However, the record does *not* begin with the Warren Court; it includes all the decisions that the Court has rendered since the Constitution itself was ratified. A clear recognition of this point is essential to a proper evaluation of the role of judicial interventionism in American government.

In writing this book, I took advantage of the unique talents of many people. Lino Graglia, Dennis Patterson, H. Jefferson Powell, and Girardeau Spann were particularly generous with their time and insights. At the University Press of Kansas, Fred Woodward provided indispensable guidance and support, and Cindy Ingham's copyediting greatly improved the final product. The secretarial staff at Rutgers Law School also rendered invaluable assistance. Finally, my wife, Peggy, and my children, David, Jonathan, and Elizabeth, provide a constant reminder that there are more important things in life than constitutional theory.

Parts of this book have been published previously in article form. Much of chapter 1 is adapted from Earl M. Maltz, "The Prospects for a Revival of Conservative Activism in Constitutional Jurisprudence," *Georgia Law Review* 24 (1990):629–68 (reprinted by permission). A portion of chapter 5 is taken from Earl M. Maltz, "Unenumerated Rights and Originalist Methodology: A Comment on the Ninth Amendment Symposium," *Chicago-Kent Law Review* 64 (1988):981–85 © 1988. Part of chapter 6 is an updated version of Earl M. Maltz, "The Supreme Court and the Quality of Political Dialogue," *Constitutional Commentary* 5 (1988):375–91. All are reproduced with permission.

ONE

THE POLITICAL DYNAMIC
OF CONSTITUTIONAL THEORY

PLANNED PARENTHOOD OF SOUTHEASTERN PENNSYLVANIA V. CASEY AND CONTEMPORARY PERCEPTIONS OF CONSTITUTIONAL THEORY

Planned Parenthood of Southeastern Pennsylvania v. Casey[1] was one of the most eagerly awaited decisions of recent years. In *Casey*, a deeply divided Court rejected a constitutional challenge to much of the Pennsylvania Abortion Control Act but struck down a provision that required women seeking abortions to notify their husbands. Although the decision was complicated by issues of *stare decisis*, public reaction to it in many ways reflected the dynamic that has come to govern theoretical discussions of constitutional law.

First, *Casey* demonstrated the degree to which judicial interventionism has become associated with liberalism in American political culture. The decision was typically described as moderately conservative. In one sense, this description might be viewed as reasonably accurate: the prochoice challenge to the Pennsylvania law generally represented the left center and left of the American political spectrum, and the Court did not hold that the Constitution required other branches of government to fully embrace that position. In another sense, however, the decision clearly favored liberal values. No member of the Court argued that states were *required* to impose the restrictions on abortion favored by many conservatives; at most, the justices concluded that states would be allowed to impose such restrictions *if they chose to do so*. By contrast, the majority explicitly prohibited the states from placing some limitations on abortion that are generally favored by conservatives and opposed by liberals. Thus, while admittedly not favoring the liberal position to the same extent as earlier decisions such as *Thornburgh v. American College of Obstetricians and Gynecologists*[2] and *City of Akron v. Akron Center for Reproductive Health*,[3] the rule announced in *Casey* nonetheless deployed the Constitution against conservative interests.

The response to *Casey* also reflected a second, closely related phenomenon: the decline in importance of the concept of judicial deference in discussions of constitutional law. Commentators focused primarily on the relationship of the restrictions allowed by the Court to the substantive positions taken by prochoice and prolife groups; they rarely (if ever) mentioned the possibility that the Court should not intervene simply because it was not the appropriate forum to mediate between the prochoice and prolife positions. The reaction of the *Philadelphia Inquirer* was typical; it declared *Casey* a "good decision" because it "meshes with what most Americans think."[4]

These two themes—the association of interventionism with liberalism and the decline of deference as an independent value—pervade much of the literature on constitutional theory. They reveal a dynamic driven by a combination of complex historical and political forces.

THE POLITICAL DYNAMIC

To understand the political dynamic that currently governs debates over judicial review, one must begin with the constitutional revolution of 1937. For roughly the first third of the twentieth century the Supreme Court had been a bastion of conservatism, interposing the Constitution as a barrier to economic regulation by both the federal and state governments. The symbol of the Court's attitude was the decision in *Lochner v. New York*,[5] in which the Court struck down a New York law limiting the number of hours that bakers might work.

Contemporary conservative theorists such as Christopher G. Tiedman defended this brand of judicial interventionism as an antidote to "democratic absolutism," necessary in order "to protect private rights against the radical experimentations of social reformers."[6] Tiedman's analysis, however, was by no means universally accepted; the Court's interventionism during the *Lochner* era drew criticism from a number of different quarters. Some of the criticism was cast in overtly ideological terms. For example, the American Federation of Labor asserted that "what confronts the workers of America . . . is . . . a series of adjudications of the highest tribunal of the land, successively destroying a basic right or cherished acquisition of organized labor, each forming a link in a fateful chain consciously designed to enslave the workers of America."[7]

More often, however, the critics of the Court during the *Lochner* era relied on institutional arguments. They contended that the Court was going beyond the proper bounds of the judicial function and usurping the powers of the legislature. For example, one commentator asserted that

it was never intended, nor is it ever necessary, that on questions of fact and of necessity and where the legislatures, acting within their special domain, have fairly and clearly spoken, the courts should oppose their ideas and their judgments to those of the popular assemblies. The members of the legislature come from the people. They can appoint committees and they can investigate. Usually they are practical men of affairs. It would seem that their opinions and judgments upon a question of fact and expediency are as reliable as those of the more or less cloistered judges. They, at any rate, are acting within the scope of their general jurisdiction.[8]

The attacks on the Court's approach escalated sharply with the advent of the Great Depression and the election of Franklin Delano Roosevelt to the presidency.[9] Congress approved a series of Roosevelt-inspired initiatives— the New Deal—which dramatically increased the role of the federal government in regulating the economy. The Supreme Court struck down a number of these initiatives.[10] Not surprisingly, Roosevelt and his adherents responded with strong criticisms of the Court, couched in both ideological and institutional terms.

The efforts of those who had opposed *Lochner*-style jurisprudence came to fruition in 1937. Changing course sharply, a majority of the Court began to consistently reject constitutional challenges to economic regulations adopted by state and federal legislatures.[11] Within five years the victory of the liberal forces was consolidated, as Roosevelt appointed a number of justices who were both ideologically committed to the New Deal and vigorously opposed to the judicial interventionism of the *Lochner* era.

While the 1937 revolution was largely a product of ideologically based objections to judicial intervention in support of conservative policies, institutional considerations also drove the post-1937 Court to generally eschew liberal as well as conservative interventionism.[12] The vast majority of judges, lawyers, and law professors have a strong commitment to the concept of "neutral principles" or some variation thereof—the idea that judicial decisionmaking should be based on some principle or set of principles that transcend the specific issue presented to the court.[13] A constitutional jurisprudence that dictated the Court should always favor the liberal position would be entirely inconsistent with this ideological viewpoint. By contrast, a principle that the Court should defer generally to legislative judgments has no obvious political bias and therefore fits comfortably within the basic framework of neutral principles. Moreover, such a principle also had great appeal on a strictly institutional level to some who, like Justice Holmes, might not be deeply committed to the liberal political program.[14] Thus it is not surprising that deference became the doctrinal basis for the Court's immediate post-1937 jurisprudence.

An emphasis on the institutional value of deference dominated academic commentary through the 1950s and 1960s.[15] On the Court itself, however, other ideological forces began to undermine the commitment to deference. Given the instrument of judicial review, the Court is inevitably the repository of considerable political power. The decision to defer is in essence a decision not to use that power—to allow instead other governmental actors final decisionmaking authority. From a purely political perspective, deference is defensible only if it seems likely that judicial interventionism will provoke an equally effective interventionist response from those holding opposing ideological views; otherwise, in political terms judicial interventionism is costless. Thus, liberal interventionism was likely to remain in check only so long as one of two related conditions prevailed: either liberals lacked a majority on the Court, or they were restrained by a fear that undue interventionism would generate a conservative backlash.

The electoral politics of the mid-twentieth century nearly guaranteed the rise of a liberal majority on the Court. From 1932 to 1968, Democrats held the presidency for all but the eight Eisenhower years and thus controlled appointments to the Court. While many of the early Democratic appointees—perhaps most notably Felix Frankfurter—were obviously haunted by the ghost of *Lochner* throughout their careers, as time passed the fear of a revival of conservative interventionism diminished and with it went one of the key factors restraining the Court. Further, the decision in *Brown v. Board of Education of Topeka*[16] in 1954 demonstrated to many liberals that judicial interventionism need not be a negative force in governmental affairs.

It is thus not surprising that in the immediate post-*Brown* era, a new style of interventionism began to emerge from the Court. Ironically, two Eisenhower appointees—Earl Warren[17] and William J. Brennan[18]—became important long-term supporters of liberal interventionism. From the mid-fifties onward they were frequently allied with William O. Douglas and Hugo L. Black. Douglas abandoned his previously restrained posture[19] to become the leading exponent of liberal interventionism on the Court,[20] and Black's unswerving commitment to the imposition of the Bill of Rights on state action[21] and absolutist view of the First Amendment[22] often led him into the liberal camp. When these four were able to garner one or more additional votes, they were successful in constitutionalizing values associated with liberal ideology.[23] With the appointment of Arthur J. Goldberg in 1962, a solidly liberal, interventionist majority was complete. This base was further strengthened by the addition of Thurgood Marshall to the Court in 1966 and remained intact through most of the 1960s. The result was that during that decade a majority of the Court found increasingly often that liberal values were guaranteed by the Constitution on a wide variety of issues ranging from criminal procedure[24] to voting rights[25] and the right to use contraceptives.[26]

The political tide began to turn against liberal interventionism in 1968. During his successful presidential campaign, Richard Nixon strongly denounced the Court's approach to constitutional adjudication, focusing particularly on issues of criminal procedure. He did not, however, pledge to appoint justices committed to actively advancing conservative values; instead, he advocated "judicial conservatism"—a constitutional jurisprudence of restraint.[27]

This strategy was influenced by several different factors. First, by emphasizing the institutional importance of restraint rather than the need to promote conservative values, Nixon and his allies could accuse their adversaries of politicizing the Court—a charge that had a powerful emotive appeal and drew substantial support from the leading academics of the day. Moreover, in 1968 a revival of conservative interventionism seemed unthinkable; fifteen years of Warren Court jurisprudence had created the strong impression that interventionism would inevitably be associated with the furtherance of liberal values. Finally, advocacy of conservative interventionism would have opened Nixon to the charge that he was urging a return to the *Lochner* era. Thus, for conservatives in the late 1960s, the philosophy of judicial restraint had many advantages and few apparent drawbacks.

Despite his victories in 1968 and 1972, Nixon was only partially successful in stemming the tide of judicial interventionism. He appointed four justices—Warren E. Burger, Harry A. Blackmun, Lewis F. Powell, and William H. Rehnquist. In addition, Gerald Ford, first Nixon's vice-president and then his successor, appointed John Paul Stevens to the Court. Of these five, only Burger and Rehnquist proved reliable adherents to the judicial philosophy espoused by Nixon. Blackmun and Stevens became frequent allies of holdover liberals Brennan and Marshall,[28] while Powell became something of a "swing" vote.[29] Consequently, the results of constitutional adjudication in the 1970s and early 1980s were somewhat mixed. The Burger Court was generally restrained in cases involving such issues as criminal procedure, education,[30] and welfare.[31] By contrast, the Court exhibited substantial liberal interventionist tendencies on a number of matters including abortion rights[32] and discrimination on the basis of gender,[33] legitimacy,[34] and alienage.[35]

Roe v. Wade[36] was particularly important. In striking down all existing state laws restricting abortions, the decision created a political firestorm, elevating the abortion debate to the status of a pressing national issue. The prolife groups, who strongly urged the overruling of *Roe*, became an important element in the conservative political coalition that controlled the Republican party.[37] The prochoice position, by contrast, was a critical part of the ideology of the feminist movement, which was a major force in the more liberal Democratic party.[38] Feminists sought not only to preserve and expand *Roe* but also to have the Court take an even more aggressive stance on issues related to gender discrimination.[39] Thus, the concept of judicial interventionism became even more closely associated with liberal ideology. Conversely, political conservatism became even more closely connected with the idea of judicial restraint.

The electoral victories of Ronald Reagan in 1980 and 1984 assured the appointment of Supreme Court justices who would share the basic conservative approach to constitutional adjudication. The dynamic on the Court, however, remained largely unaltered until near the end of the Reagan presidency. Reagan appointed a total of three new justices. The first two—Sandra Day O'Connor, replacing Potter Stewart, and Antonin Scalia, replacing Warren Burger—produced only slight changes in the Court's direction; in each case, the conservative Reagan appointee took the seat of a justice who had often opposed liberal interventionism. By contrast, the replacement of Powell by Anthony M. Kennedy effected a dramatic shift in the balance of power on the Court. Kennedy often joined with Rehnquist, O'Connor, Scalia, and holdover Byron White to create a majority in opposition to calls for liberal interventionism.[40] George Bush continued the trend, appointing conservatives David H. Souter and Clarence Thomas to replace Brennan and Marshall, respectively. The political transformation of the Court was then complete, and the liberal interventionist tone of the judiciary has continued to become more muted.

By contrast, the commentators have moved in the opposite direction from the Court itself. Rather than criticizing the Court for going beyond its proper function, liberal constitutional theorists (long the dominant voice in the academy) have increasingly adopted theories that seek to justify judicial interventionism. This change may reflect not only the wedding of conservatism and the concept of judicial restraint but also the institutional momentum generated by over a quarter century of judicial interventionism. For these or other reasons, many liberal academics have chosen to emphasize the benefits to be derived from an interventionist judiciary rather than focus on the institutional values of restraint.

In taking this view, liberal theorists have embraced a methodology that is in essence the mirror image of the traditional conservative analysis. They put forth a seemingly neutral vision of the role of the courts and then attempt to demonstrate that their model compels the adoption of a variety of liberal positions. One popular approach is to urge the courts to enforce some general "theme" arising from the constitutional structure rather than specific intentions of the drafters of the Constitution. For example, David A. J. Richards designates "toleration" as the central focus of American constitutional development,[41] while Judith A. Baer argues that the Fourteenth Amendment is a "lavish grant of liberty and equality."[42] Other liberal theorists, such as Owen Fiss and Michael J. Perry, have argued that the judiciary is peculiarly well-suited to advance the moral development of society through constitutional adjudication.[43] In each case, the theorist concludes by arguing that his or her theory requires judicial intervention in favor of certain left/center positions.

Other, more radical academics have carried the attack on noninterventionism even further. Viewing judicial review as purely political in the same sense that legislative action is purely political, these commentators call upon the Court to use the Constitution as a device to promote various radical political programs. While some, such as Mark V. Tushnet and Richard L. Parker, focus their attention on wide-ranging questions of inequality in American society,[44] others consider specific problems. Critical race theorists such as Richard Delgado and Mari J. Matsuda advocate an aggressive judicial assault on all vestiges of racism in American society;[45] feminist scholars including Robin West and Christine A. Littleton argue for a vigorous attack on laws and institutions that support differentiation in sex roles.[46] All, however, are united in their disdain for the claim that institutional constraints should play a central role in the Court's decisionmaking process.

The increasing commitment of liberal and radical constitutional theorists to judicial interventionism is revealed in the reactions of the academy to *Roe* and *Bowers v. Hardwick*,[47] respectively. Not surprisingly, at the time *Roe* was decided, some prochoice academics fervently defended the decision.[48] But even some prochoice theorists were troubled by the Court's action. For example, while expressing their support for the basic concept of legalized abortion, Harry H. Wellington and John Hart Ely condemned the *Roe* decision itself, arguing that in constitutionalizing the abortion question the Court had stepped outside the bounds of the appropriate judicial function.[49]

The pattern of commentary that followed the *Bowers* decision thirteen years later stands in stark contrast to the diversity of the response to *Roe*. In *Bowers*, the majority relied heavily on institutional arguments—particularly on the importance of deference—in refusing to strike down a Georgia statute that outlawed homosexual sodomy. Commentators have almost unanimously condemned the decision.[50] Some have criticized the judgment as resting on either "homophobic" or inherently "conservative" political assumptions.[51] Others have maintained that the Court should have adopted an explicitly antihomophobic posture.[52] In neither case have the critics been willing to consider the idea of deference as a general value with independent worth.

In the political arena, the hearings on the nomination of Robert H. Bork to the Supreme Court also reflected the degree to which liberal thinkers have abandoned the concept of judicial deference. Bork was defeated because his opponents were successful in portraying him as "an extremist who would use his position on the Court to Advance [sic] a far-right, radical judicial agenda."[53] The primary evidence offered to support this charge was not that Bork would use a seat on the Supreme Court to overturn left/center initiatives from other branches of government; indeed, Bork has been outspoken in his opposition to the use of judicial power to invalidate economic legislation that might well be anathema to conservatives.[54] Instead, the label of "extremism" was based on the likelihood that Bork would be unwilling to actively oppose legislation that left/center forces found distasteful, most notably on matters dealing with contraception, abortion, and gender discrimination.[55] The subsequent nomination of Justice Kennedy was approved only because some of those who opposed Bork believed that Kennedy might be more receptive to liberal arguments on these issues.[56] In neither case was the suggestion that deference might not necessarily denote a conservative political posture taken seriously by liberal politicians.

In short, conservative theorists have not succeeded in convincing their left/center counterparts or the polity at large of the desirability of basing constitutional theory on the concept of deference. Because left/center analysts have come to equate this seemingly neutral concept with the conservative political philosophy, they have rejected any recommendation that the Supreme Court take a basically noninterventionist approach in constitutional adjudication. Equally important, the public reaction to the Bork controversy seemed to indicate that the general populace had become inured to the idea of judicial interventionism as well.

The fact that nonconservatives tend to dismiss the models based on originalism or deference would certainly be viewed as unfortunate by those committed to such models for institutional reasons; they would, however, consider it largely irrelevant to their own approach to constitutional analysis. By contrast, the situation poses a much more real and immediate *political* dilemma for mainstream conservative theorists. As long as conservatives generally adhere to the originalist/deference model, the judiciary will generally be neutral when conservatives control the courts—neutral at least in the sense that judges will allow liberal political initiatives adopted by other branches to survive constitutional challenges. But as long as nonconservatives reject this model in favor of an interventionist approach, when left/center forces control the judiciary, courts will invalidate a substantial number of conservative political initiatives. The result is that in the long run, courts will always on balance be an anticonservative political force in society.

Given the refusal of left/center politicians, scholars, and judges to accept the argument for deference, the political problems faced by conservatives when dealing with the judiciary could have only one solution—the development of a theory of conservative interventionism. In simple terms, conservative judges would use constitutional adjudication as a vehicle to thwart left/center initiatives from other branches, just as left/center judges have used constitutional adjudication to thwart conservative initiatives. A theory of conservative interventionism would abandon the supposition that judges should play a neutral role between competing political forces; instead, it would recognize that depending on the ideological predilections of the justices of the Supreme Court, at any given time the judiciary would favor one political camp or the other. Over the long term, however, the sum total of judicial interventionism might well be politically neutral, as the personnel of the courts and their impact on policy decisions shift with the ebb and flow of the political tide.

Given this political context, it is not surprising that some scholars such as Richard A. Epstein,[57] Randy E. Barnett,[58] Stephen Macedo,[59] and Bernard H. Siegan[60] have begun to develop theoretical frameworks to defend conservative interventionism. Some of the new nonoriginalist justifications mirror the arguments that have made constitutional interventionism a staple of left/center constitutional theory. Barnett and Macedo, for example, argue for an open-ended view of the Ninth Amendment, while Siegan focuses on the due process clauses of the Fifth and Fourteenth amendments. Epstein, by contrast, relies primarily on the takings and contracts clauses, which have been out of favor with most left/center theorists. Despite their differences, all come to the same basic conclusion—that the Supreme Court should intervene to prevent undue interference with the operation of the free enterprise system.

The influence of the conservative interventionist movement has begun to be felt on the Supreme Court itself. In recent years, interventionist decisions reflecting conservative ideology can be found on issues ranging from freedom of speech to the protection of property rights and race-based affirmative action. Further, even when the Court's majority has rejected calls for conservative interventionism, dissents have become increasingly common. Depending on the particular context, conservative interventionists have achieved their goals by either co-opting the analysis of existing caselaw or departing substantially from the approach taken by the Warren Court.

TURNING LIBERAL DOCTRINE TO CONSERVATIVE ENDS: THE CASE OF THE FIRST AMENDMENT

The First Amendment provides the most dramatic example of the use of doctrines developed by liberal interventionists in the service of conservative political ideology. During the Warren and Burger years, the jurisprudence of free speech was marked by two characteristics. First, more liberal elements on the Court strongly resisted efforts to regulate speech based on its offensiveness. For example, over the dissents of newly appointed justices Burger and Blackmun (as well as Justice Black), the Court held in *Cohen v. California*[61] that the state of California could not constitutionally punish a Vietnam War protester for wearing a jacket bearing the words "Fuck the Draft" in a courtroom. Speaking for the majority, John Marshall Harlan argued that "while the particular four-letter word being litigated here is perhaps more distasteful than most others of its genre, it is nevertheless often true that one man's vulgarity is another's lyric. Indeed, we think it is largely because governmental officials cannot make principled distinctions in this area that the Constitution leaves matters of taste and style so largely to the individual."[62]

Second, this period's liberal approach to the First Amendment entailed a willingness to provide strong protection for "symbolic speech"—actions that are intended to convey a political or ideological message. Thus, in *Clark v. Community for Creative Non-Violence*,[63] Brennan and Marshall argued that the National Park Service was constitutionally required to grant a permit allowing demonstrators seeking to dramatize the plight of the homeless to sleep in Lafayette Park.[64]

During the early Rehnquist era, these two elements came together in *Texas v. Johnson*.[65] In *Johnson*, a person who had publicly burned an American flag as a political protest was convicted under a statute that made it illegal to "deface, damage, or otherwise physically mistreat [the flag] in a way that the actor knows will seriously offend one or more persons likely to observe or discover his action." A majority of the Court in *Johnson* found that this conviction violated the First Amendment. Speaking for the Court, Justice Brennan noted that the protester could not have been punished for innocently mistreating the flag and rested his argument on the "bedrock principle underlying the First Amendment . . . that the Government may not prohibit the expression of an idea simply because society finds the idea itself offensive or disagreeable."[66]

Not surprisingly, the Court's decision in *Johnson* was strongly supported by liberal commentators[67] and opposed by many prominent conservatives.[68] On the Court itself, however, the ideological mix was much more complex. Without the votes of Scalia and Kennedy—usually two of the most conservative justices of the Rehnquist Court—Johnson's conviction would have been upheld. If *Johnson* were to be considered alone, the position of Scalia and Kennedy might be interpreted simply as a reflection of a libertarian strand in conservative thought. The subsequent decision in *R.A.V. v. St. Paul*,[69] however, cast their vote in a somewhat different light.

In *R.A.V.*, the Court unanimously reversed a conviction for burning a cross under a city ordinance that prohibited the display of offensive symbols "which one . . . has reasonable grounds to know arouses anger, alarm, or resentment in others on the basis of race, color, creed, religion, or gender." On purely doctrinal ground, the case would have been difficult to distinguish from *Johnson*; the content of the message conveyed in *R.A.V.* was clearly necessary to the conviction, and the communicative effect of burning a cross is the same as that of burning an American flag. On one level, then, the Court's decision was hardly surprising.

What was rather startling about *R.A.V.* was the breakdown of the vote. Four justices were content merely to reverse the conviction on the basis that the ordinance was unconstitutionally overbroad.[70] Yet the five most conservative members of the Court—Rehnquist, Scalia, Kennedy, Souter, and Thomas—all joined an opinion by Scalia phrased in far more sweeping terms. Scalia argued that even so-called fighting words may not be regulated "based on hostility—or favoritism—toward the underlying message expressed" and that "the First Amendment does not permit [government] to impose special prohibitions on those speakers who express views on disfavored subjects."[71]

This voting pattern becomes understandable in view of the emerging national debate over political correctness. During the 1980s, an increasing number of colleges and universities enacted codes of conduct prohibiting speech that cast aspersions on individuals or groups based on race, gender, or sexual preference. The constituencies that had generally supported Warren Court–style interventionism were split on the desirability and constitutionality of these restrictive codes. Many traditional liberals, led by the American Civil Liberties Union, strongly condemned the prohibitions;[72] other firm advocates of judicial protection for minority groups defended the codes of conduct.[73] Conservatives, in contrast, were united in their opposition to the restrictions.[74]

Given this political context, the eagerness of the conservative members of the Rehnquist Court to denounce content-based regulations of speech becomes easily understandable. By throwing the mantle of the First Amendment around cross burning—a form of symbolic speech with a particularly reprehensible pedigree—Justice Scalia sent a clear signal that the majority would tolerate none of the restrictions on speech imposed by the academic codes of conduct.[75] Thus Scalia was able to use liberal interventionist doctrine as a device to support the conservative political agenda.

CHANGING THE DOCTRINAL FRAMEWORK: THE REINVIGORATION OF CONSTITUTIONAL PROTECTION FOR PROPERTY RIGHTS

In one important sense, the decision in *R.A.V.* is something of an aberration; usually, the doctrinal basis for liberal interventionist decisions is not easily adaptable to the conservative political program. More often, conservative interventionism has required at the very least a change in the orientation of existing doctrine. The Court's recent treatment of the constitutional status of property rights is an excellent case in point.

Although the hallmark of *Lochner*-era jurisprudence was its emphasis on private property and freedom of contract, conventional property rights received relatively little substantive protection from the Supreme Court during the period from 1937 to 1977. The first hint of a reversal in this trend came in *United States Trust Co. of New York v. New Jersey*[76] and *Allied Structural*

Steel v. Spannaus,[77] where the Court invoked the contracts clause to invalidate state legislation that retroactively changed the contractual rights and obligations of contracting parties. While these decisions did not presage the reemergence of the contracts clause as a major force in constitutional jurisprudence, they did reflect the determination of some justices to protect property rights.

More recently, the Court's weapon of choice has been the takings clause, which provides that the government cannot take private property without compensation. From the revolution of 1937 through the Warren era, the Court was generally unsympathetic to challenges based on the takings clause. Despite repeatedly proclaiming its adherence to the view that takings issues would depend "upon the particular circumstances [of each] case,"[78] in practice the justices of that era rarely found in favor of the property owner.[79] Lately, however, both academic commentators and the more conservative members of the Court have shown increasing interest in using the takings clause not only against physical invasions of property[80] but also against so-called regulatory takings.[81] The evolution of the Court's approach to the latter issue illustrates well the substantial changes that have transformed the dynamic governing judicial interventionism.

Indications of a possible shift in the Court's position on regulatory takings could be detected as early as 1978 in *Penn Central Transportation Co. v. City of New York*.[82] In that case, the Court rejected a constitutional challenge to a zoning ordinance that prevented a corporate landowner from using the airspace above its property. However, the majority opinion provoked a strong dissent from three justices—all Republican appointees—who argued that the ordinance was an uncompensated taking of the owner's property. Obviously, if the *Penn Central* dissenters could gain ideological allies on the Court, then the takings clause might become a significant barrier to economic regulations.

By 1987, Chief Justice Burger had been replaced by Antonin Scalia and Justice Stewart by Sandra Day O'Connor. The net effect of these appointments was to bump the Court at least marginally to the right in takings cases, leaving the balance of power in the hands of "swing" justices such as Powell and White. The new decisionmaking dynamic was revealed in *Keystone Bituminous Coal Association v. DeBenedictus*[83] and *Nollan v. California Coastal Commission*.[84] In *DeBenedictus*, the Court rejected a challenge to a Pennsylvania law requiring that 50 percent of the coal beneath certain structures be left in place in order to prevent damage to those structures caused by "subsidence"—the lowering of the strata overlying a coal mine. In

Nollan, by contrast, the Court struck down a ruling that conditioned the granting of a building permit on the owners' agreement to provide an easement allowing public access to a local beach. Both cases found the justices split five to four, with only Byron White voting one way in *Nollan* and another in *DeBenedictus*. Brennan, Marshall, Blackmun, and Stevens united to reject both constitutional attacks, and Nixon appointees Powell and Rehnquist joined Reagan appointees O'Connor and Scalia in finding the challenged actions unconstitutional.

The appointment of Clarence Thomas reinforced the view that the Constitution should be interpreted so as to furnish substantial protection for property rights. The decision in *Lucas v. South Carolina Coastal Council*[85] illustrated the depth of the support for this position on the Court. *Lucas* dealt with the claim of a landowner who had purchased beachfront property with the intent to build houses there. Subsequent to his purchase, the property was declared part of an environmentally fragile area, and the landowner was prohibited from building on the property. Six members of the Court concluded that the state regulation constituted a taking of the property and that compensation was therefore required. Speaking for the Court, Antonin Scalia declared that "when the owner of real property has been called upon to sacrifice *all* economically beneficial uses in the name of common good . . . he has suffered a taking."[86] Thus, as in *R.A.V.*, a majority of the Court showed its willingness to deploy the Constitution in support of conservative values.

The current practical impact of the new conservative interventionism should not be overstated. The concept of judicial restraint remains an important element of conservative political thought;[87] moreover, the inertia generated by the existing structure of constitutional law virtually guarantees that, on balance, interventionist decisions will still be much more likely to favor liberal than conservative ideology.[88] Nonetheless, decisions such as *R.A.V.* and *Lucas* clearly belie any suggestion that interventionism is necessarily associated with left or left/center political thought, either in theory or practice. Instead, discussions of constitutional analysis must begin with the premise that judicial interventionism might conceivably support an array of different political positions.

TWO
ORIGINALISM AND ITS CRITICS

Analysis of a jurisprudence based on the original understanding is a logical starting place for a general discussion of constitutional theory. Despite repeated declarations of its demise by opponents, originalism continues to play a central role in the debate over the proper structure of constitutional law. Originalists such as Raoul Berger[1] and Robert H. Bork[2] remain by any standard major voices in the debate. Moreover, originalism is an important factor in most nonoriginalist theory as well, since nonoriginalists typically begin with a recitation of the perceived shortcomings of a jurisprudence rooted in the original understanding. Originalism also provides a convenient baseline against which other approaches can be measured. Finally, many of those who reject a strict reliance on the original understanding retain originalist elements as part of their overall framework.

CRITERIA FOR EVALUATION

One of the principal difficulties involved in analyzing originalism (or any other theory of constitutional adjudication) is that there is no consensus on the criteria for evaluating constitutional theories. One prominent group of modern scholars takes what might be described as a linguistic approach to the problem. Proponents of the linguistic model note that nearly all constitutional theorists see the problem in terms of interpreting a written document—the Constitution. They conclude that the debate over constitutional theory should therefore be guided by the insights of other disciplines such as literary criticism and the philosophy of language, which also examine the question of how recorded language should be interpreted. Beginning with this perspective, they often defend nonoriginalist interventionism.[3]

Linguistic analysis is ultimately unpersuasive because it obscures important aspects of constitutional theory. Admittedly, constitutional analysis does purport to provide a method for interpreting a written document. Constitutional interpretation is not, however, an abstract or aesthetic exercise. Instead, as Judge Richard Posner has reminded us, the task is to define the role of the courts in determining the powers of government and the relationship of governmental units to the citizenry and to one other. This task is quintessentially political; thus it is political theory that serves as the appropriate benchmark against which any method of constitutional interpretation must be tested.[4]

At the opposite end of the spectrum from commentators who embrace linguistic analysis are the radical theorists who have adopted an approach that might be described as the theory of pure politics. Adherents to this theory deny that decisions of the Court should be measured against some distinctively legal standard. Instead, they contend that the decisions should be viewed simply as expressions of public policy and should be evaluated accordingly. Advocates of the purely political viewpoint rest their case on two observations. First, they note that the constitutional decisions of the Supreme Court often deal with issues—such as abortion, desegregation, and affirmative action—that are clearly political in nature. Second, they observe that in controversial cases, the position of the justices is often (if not invariably) determined by their personal political philosophy rather than some legal theory applicable only to judges.

Many of the insights that inform the theory of pure politics are admittedly indispensable to a proper understanding of the role of the Supreme Court in American society. However, even if actual decisions were never influenced by institutional concerns, the theory of pure politics would not necessarily be the appropriate starting point for constitutional analysis. Most constitutional theorists do not view their work as entirely or even primarily descriptive. Instead, constitutional theories typically have a strong normative element, either justifying existing judicial practices or advocating changes in those practices. Of course, even from a normative perspective one might urge that judges in constitutional cases should simply follow their political preferences—a view that would eliminate the need for an independent theory of constitutional adjudication. Most commentators, however, believe that these preferences should be modified or displaced by legal conventions peculiar to the process of constitutional adjudication.

Confronting this argument directly, theorists such as Mark Tushnet argue that it is impossible to construct a theory of constitutional adjudication that will act as a meaningful constraint on the judicial decisionmaking process. If this contention were correct, it would essentially end the debate over constitutional theory. However, as the actual voting pattern of the justices demonstrates, Tushnet's position is much overstated.

The jurisprudence of Antonin Scalia yields an instructive case study. Scalia is generally associated with the strongly conservative wing of American political thought, and his voting record on the Court is replete with examples of the influence of this conservatism. Nonetheless, his approach also reflects the importance of other, institutional concerns—most notably, an overarching commitment to judicial deference and to a regime of specific rules rather than broad guidelines. The impact of these concerns is evident in Scalia's approach to both statutory interpretation and constitutional adjudication.

In the statutory context, his opinion in *United Auto Workers v. Johnson Controls, Inc.*[5] is particularly striking. *Johnson Controls* was a challenge to an employer's policy of prohibiting fertile women from working in positions that would potentially expose fetuses to high doses of lead. A number of employees attacked this policy under the Civil Rights Act of 1964, which prohibits discrimination on the basis of sex, and the Pregnancy Discrimination Act, which prohibits discrimination against pregnant women.

The employer's position implicitly combined elements of prolife ideology with a more general appeal to the concept of employer autonomy; as such, in the abstract one might expect it to be especially attractive to someone of Justice Scalia's political bent. Nonetheless, Scalia rejected the employer's arguments. His strongly worded opinion disclosed the powerful institutional considerations that dictated his conclusions: "By reason of the Pregnancy Discrimination Act, it would not matter if all pregnant women placed their children at risk in taking these jobs. . . . Title VII gives parents the power to make occupational decisions affecting their families. A legislative forum is available to those who believe such decisions should be made elsewhere."[6]

Given decisions such as *Johnson Controls*, one can hardly argue that properly designed institutional constraints would not have a significant effect on judicial decisionmaking. At this point, however, one might expect to confront the argument that constitutional analysis is fundamentally different from statutory interpretation, making institutional considerations inherently less important. Admittedly, the Court has in practice been less constrained in constitutional cases, particularly where highly charged political issues are involved. For example, it is difficult to explain Scalia's position on race-based affirmative action in any terms other than pure politics.[7] At the same time, however, there is no *theoretical* reason why strong institutional constraints might not be imposed in constitutional cases. Indeed, the impact of such constraints is evident in Scalia's analysis of dormant commerce clause cases.

As already noted, a distaste for government regulation of business is one of the central tenets of conservative thought. Dormant commerce clause cases provide an important opportunity to limit such government regulation, because the question in these cases is whether a particular state regulation constitutes an unacceptable burden on interstate business. Therefore, if ordinary determinations of policy were the only consideration, one would expect Scalia to take a strongly interventionist stance in commerce clause cases.

In fact, however, Scalia has been generally hostile to commerce clause claims. Dismissing the balancing approach that has dominated modern commerce clause jurisprudence—an analysis under which a justice, if so inclined, could easily justify a wide range of interventions—Scalia instead consistently argues that the dormant commerce clause invalidates state regulations if and only if such regulations either discriminate against out-of-state businesses or seek to directly control out-of-state activities. Thus, although Scalia doubted the economic benefits of a state antitakeover statute in *CTS Corp. v. Dynamics Corp. of America*,[8] he rejected a constitutional challenge to the statute, noting that "a law can be both economic folly and constitutional."[9]

The central question in constitutional theory is whether similar strong constraints should be applied by *all* justices on *all* constitutional issues and, if so, what the content of those constraints should be. The appropriate point of departure for this inquiry is an analysis of originalism—the philosophy that purports to impose the most stringent constraints of any modern approach to constitutional analysis.

ORIGINALISM AND INTERVENTIONISM

Most discussions of the efficacy of an originalist approach to judicial review have been shaped by the premise that originalism is synonymous with noninterventionism. As Robert W. Bennett has noted, this assumption is fatally flawed.[10] Admittedly, from an originalist perspective the Tenth Amendment does operate as an important restraint on the freedom of action of the federal courts—a point whose significance will be explored later in greater detail. Adoption of originalism does not, however, amount to a complete renunciation of judicial interventionism.

Some of the interventionism required by a pure originalist analysis would no doubt be applauded even by left/center constitutional theorists. For example, even under the narrowest view of the original understanding of the First Amendment and the Reconstruction amendments, the Court would be required to provide *some* protection for freedom of speech and the rights of racial minorities, respectively. The degree of interventionism mandated by originalism on these matters would no doubt be insufficient to satisfy the desires of left/center theorists, but the results would nonetheless be clearly distinguishable from a stringently noninterventionist regime.

Further, originalist analysis would support interventionism in some areas where left/center theorists have typically been strong advocates of judicial deference. Among the best examples are such provisions as the contracts clause and the takings clause of the Fifth Amendment, which were plainly understood to render substantial protection for the rights of property holders and other members of the wealthier classes. One might legitimately debate the precise scope of the original understanding of the protections provided by these clauses; it is certain, however, that they were intended to place some significant restraints on government action.

Finally, from a pure originalist perspective the Tenth Amendment itself mandates a considerable degree of judicial interventionism—in some circumstances, an interventionism far more wide-ranging than that advocated by other currently popular models of judicial review. Issues of congressional power over the economy are particularly illustrative. Under the doctrine of enumerated powers, codified in the Tenth Amendment, Congress can take no action not affirmatively authorized by some constitutional provision. In recent years, the idea that this doctrine should be a material constraint on federal action has had more theoretical than practical significance. Using the congressional power to control "commerce among the states" as its vehicle, the Court has held that the federal government has authority to regulate all private activities that have any impact, however indirect or minimal, on the interstate market.[11] In effect, these decisions have created a regime in which the powers of the federal government are limited only by specific constitutional constraints. Further, many commentators who have been aggressively interventionist in other contexts have strongly opposed any effort that would extend the Court's reach over economic issues.

From an originalist perspective, the Court's near-total commitment to noninterventionism in this arena is defensible only if the framers believed that they were granting Congress almost unlimited authority to regulate matters affecting the economy. While some commentators have taken this view of the original understanding of the scope of the commerce clause, other scholars have concluded that the framers intended to grant Congress only the power to regulate the movement of goods and people between states. The latter conclusion is far more consistent with the drafters' repeated assurances that they were creating a federal government with strictly limited powers, leaving authority over most matters in the hands of the states. A consistent originalist would therefore advocate a significant increase in interventionism against assertions of congressional authority.

From the foregoing, it should be obvious that originalism and noninterventionism are far from synonymous. Originalists therefore cannot rely on arguments against judicial interventionism to defend their position—at least in those instances in which originalist theory itself mandates interventionism. Instead, they must put forth some justification that supports originalist intervention despite the force of arguments against interventionism generally.

ORIGINALISM AND LEGITIMATE AUTHORITY

The most plausible defense of originalism rests on a single axiom: The framers of the Constitution had legitimate authority to make political decisions that would bind future governmental decisionmakers until superseded by judgments made through the process specified in the Constitution itself. As a corollary to this premise, federal judges are required to invalidate actions inconsistent with limitations imposed by the framers. At the same time, however, where other government actors act consistently with the original understanding, the federal courts should defer to their decisions; the same legitimate authority that established the courts themselves requires judges to respect the specific grants of power to Congress and the reservation of powers to the states in the Tenth Amendment.

The gist of this argument for originalism—the legitimacy of the constitutionmaking process—is admittedly controversial. At the same time, however, it must be the starting point for any credible justification of federal judicial review. After all, the federal courts (not to mention the other branches of the federal government) owe their existence and authority to the Constitution. Thus, if the process by which the Constitution was created is illegitimate, then the federal courts can hardly claim that they have legitimate authority to strike down the actions of state governments. In short, the premise of legitimate authority must underlie any defense of judicial review—originalist or otherwise.

PRACTICAL DIFFICULTIES IN IDENTIFYING
THE ORIGINAL UNDERSTANDING

Although the premise of legitimate authority provides a sound theoretical basis for originalist theory, application of the theory presents significant practical problems.[12] Building on the seminal work of Paul A. Brest,[13] one group of nonoriginalist interventionists argues that these problems are fatal to the originalist project. Critics from this school seek to demonstrate that identification of the original understanding is by its nature an impossible task and that attempts to construct a coherent originalist theory will therefore inevitably fail. Moreover, they suggest that the necessary implication of this conclusion is that the federal courts must adopt some other, more interventionist approach to constitutional adjudication.

As a preliminary matter, it should be noted that a demonstration of the incoherence of originalism would not necessarily imply that the Supreme Court should embrace a more interventionist mode of analysis. Depending on the strength of the arguments for and against nonoriginalist interventionism, one might just as well infer that the Court should abandon judicial review altogether. Nonetheless, Brest and like-minded theorists have clearly articulated objections that any committed originalist must take seriously.

In their attacks on originalism, nonoriginalists of the Brest school typically rely on two different kinds of arguments. One set of claims focuses on the difficulty of interpreting the historical record. Brest, for example, points out that the historical record is never absolutely complete and is often fraught with ambiguities. He also notes that an originalist must translate the beliefs of the framers about the conditions of their own era into theories about modern situations that may have had no precise parallel when the relevant constitutional provision was drafted.[14] Regarding this process, Brest concludes that "the act of translation required here . . . involves the counterfactual and imaginary act of projecting the adopters' concepts and attitudes into a future they probably would not have envisioned. When the interpreter engages in this sort of projection, she is in a fantasy world more of her own than of the adopters' making."[15]

Although Brest suggests that the uncertainty created by these problems critically undermines originalist theory, he is overstating the significance of his observations. Originalist theory does not demand that an examination of the historical record yield a definite, uncontroversial answer to constitutional questions. Depending upon the political/social context in which they are operating and other factors, judges may reach divergent conclusions on the implications of the historical evidence. However, originalism requires only that each judge make a good-faith estimate of the original understanding and that his or her decisionmaking process be guided by that understanding.

A second set of criticisms is based on the ambiguities inherent in the very concept of an original understanding. For example, in addition to his other arguments, Brest notes that the original understanding to be discovered is that of a body or group of bodies as a whole. He points out, however, that the bodies themselves are made up of individuals, each of whom might have a different perception of a constitutional provision. Simple reference to "the original understanding" does not tell the judge which of many understandings should prevail.

Moreover, as Ronald Dworkin has observed, each individual might have a variety of intentions with respect to a particular provision. He argues that originalism is flawed because it fails to identify the level of abstraction at which the framers' intentions should be considered.[16] Here the equal protection clause serves as a useful example. On one level, the drafters of the clause might be said to have intended to ensure that blacks would have freedom from invidious discrimination. More generally, however, one might also plausibly contend that the drafters were concerned with guaranteeing a fair distribution of resources and that discrimination against blacks was simply the specific case that drove them to amend the Constitution. Depending on the level of abstraction considered relevant, either view might appropriately be described as the original understanding of the framers of the Fourteenth Amendment.[17]

In a certain sense, most originalist theorists have invited criticisms such as those of Brest and Dworkin. They seem to assume that one, clear, indisputable original understanding exists, and they build their arguments on this foundation. Nevertheless, the criticisms themselves do not conclusively discredit originalist theory; they do, however, expose the need for further elaboration of that theory. What is called for is what Mark Tushnet has termed "supplementary evidentiary rules"—principles to guide judges in situations where the historical record is unclear or reveals disagreements among the framers.[18]

In the abstract, these rules might take any number of different forms, with widely divergent implications for the extent of interventionism in which the Court should engage. In choosing among the possibilities, the critical factor should be the general justification for the adoption of an originalist approach—that is, the theory that the framers had legitimate authority to adopt legal rules that would bind future governmental decisionmakers and that the courts should act in a manner that vindicates this authority. The supplemental rules chosen should be consistent with this postulate.

Given this premise, the starting point for the construction of supplemental evidentiary rules should be what Brest has described as the "interpretive intent" of the framers themselves. If the framers had legitimate authority to create binding substantive constitutional norms, then they also must have had authority to establish the principles governing the interpretation of those norms. Thus, a consistent originalist should begin his or her analysis with an examination of the framers' theory of constitutional interpretation.

Historians who have studied the background of the Constitution are deeply divided on the interpretive intent of the framers. Some have concluded that the framers did not envisage arming the federal courts with the power of judicial review at all, or that they intended that such a power would be exercised only in a very limited class of cases.[19] An originalist who regarded the evidence for this assertion as persuasive would be forced to conclude that the Court should abandon judicial review in most or all situations.

Other historians take the opposing view, arguing that the framers did in fact contemplate the exercise of judicial review by the federal courts.[20] Yet these historians do not agree on which theory of constitutional interpretation the framers endorsed. Some argue that the framers embraced a "plain meaning" theory rather than accepting the original understanding as authoritative; others credit the idea that the original understanding was believed to be significant but differ on the question of *whose* understanding was thought to be authoritative.

The Plain Meaning Rule

One reputed strand of the framers' interpretive theory is completely inconsistent with originalist analysis. Both Leonard W. Levy and H. Jefferson Powell contend that an important segment of the legal community among the framers held the view that the Constitution should be given an openended reading in accordance with the plain meaning of its language.[21] As one prime example of this approach, Powell cites the arguments of the prominent antifederalist Brutus, who warned that because the Constitution's grants of authority were "conceived in general and indefinite terms, which are either equivocal, ambiguous, or which require long definitions to unfold the extent of their meaning," judges would be forced to interpret the document "according to the reasoning spirit of it, without being confined to the words or letter."[22]

Taken alone, Brutus's argument might be dismissed as simply overstated rhetoric, expressing the most extreme fears of the opponents of the Constitution rather than the intent of its framers. However, Powell and Levy also call to witness James Madison, relying on two connected facets of Madison's reasoning on constitutional interpretation. First, Madison explicitly recognized that "it could not but happen, and was foreseen at the birth of the Constitution, that difficulties and differences of opinion might occasionally arise in expounding terms and phrases necessarily used in [the Constitution] . . . and that it might require a regular course of practice to liquidate and settle the meaning of some of them."[23] Second, he regarded governmentally promulgated interpretations of constitutional provisions that had widespread public acceptance to be authoritative, even when those interpretations departed from the original understanding.[24] Thus, in Powell's words, "the Constitution is a public document, and its interpretation, for Madison, was in the end a public process."[25]

Madison's reputation as "the father of the Constitution" is not entirely deserved; as Forrest McDonald has demonstrated, the influence of Madison's thought on the drafting of the Constitution has been greatly exaggerated.[26] Nonetheless, Madison was clearly a key political figure and supporter of the Constitution once the Philadelphia convention submitted it to the states for ratification. In short, the evidence presented by Powell and Levy does suggest that the legal theory of the founding period contained important strands of nonoriginalist thought.

Levy claims that the writings of Brutus and Madison provide historical support for the brand of judicial interventionism espoused by most modern-day nonoriginalists. Taken in historical context, however, the evidence lends itself to quite different implications. Neither Brutus nor Madison was dealing with the question of the proper interpretation of the rights-creating provisions of either the original Constitution or the Bill of Rights. Instead, both were preoccupied with the scope of congressional power conferred by Article I. By embracing the notion that public acquiescence might change the parameters of Article I authority, Madison was accepting the possibility that future congresses might, in some circumstances, legitimately exercise powers not contemplated by the framers. Similarly, Brutus expressed fear that the "most natural and grammatical interpretation" of Article I, section 8, was that it authorized Congress to do "any thing which in their judgment will tend to provide for the general welfare and [that] this amounts to the same thing as general and unlimited powers of legislation in all cases."[27] Such an assessment leads to a regime of judicial review that is *less* interventionist than that envisioned by pure originalist analysis.

This point emerges clearly in Chief Justice John Marshall's well-known opinion in *McCulloch v. Maryland*,[28] the most prominent early judicial defense of an open-ended view of the Constitution. Marshall was faced with a challenge to the constitutionality of congressional action chartering the Second National Bank of the United States, based on the fact that Article I does not explicitly grant Congress the power to charter a bank. Nonetheless, Marshall rejected the challenge, declaring that "we must never forget that it is a constitution we are expounding" and that "its nature . . . requires . . . that only its great outlines should be marked, its important objects designated, and the minor ingredients which compose those objects be deduced from the nature of the objects themselves."[29]

Advocates of open-ended interventionism often cite *McCulloch* to support their position. In fact, however, Marshall was deploying his theory of congressional interpretation *against* a plea for judicial interventionism—in other words, to justify rejection of a constitutional challenge to congressional action. Marshall was clearly cognizant of this point, noting that "the sound construction of the constitution must allow to the . . . legislature that discretion . . . which will enable [it] to perform the high duties assigned to it."[30] Moreover, the existence of specific limitations on congressional authority mitigated against an interventionist approach that would impose substantial additional constraints on congressional power.[31] Thus, taken as a whole, the *McCulloch* opinion stands as a powerful argument in favor of judicial restraint—the antithesis of the position taken by modern nonoriginalist interventionists.

Supporters of nonoriginalist interventionism can, however, draw on some late eighteenth-century interpretations of *state* constitutions to support their view of the original understanding of interpretive principles. Spencer Roane's opinion in *Kamper v. Hawkins*[32] is a prominent example. *Kamper* was a challenge to a Virginia statute that sought to assign equity judges extensive new duties in common law cases. While Roane concludes that the statute was unconstitutional, his description of the proper scope of judicial review bears a striking similarity to the arguments of modern-day judicial interventionists:

The Judiciary may and ought to adjudge a law unconstitutional and void, if it be plainly repugnant to the letter of the Constitution *or the fundamental principles thereof*. By fundamental principles I understand, those great principles growing out of the Constitution, by the aid of which, in dubious cases, the Constitution may be explained and preserved inviolate; those land-marks, which it may be necessary to resort

to, on account of the impossibility to foresee or provide for cases within
the spirit, but without the letter of the Constitution.[33]

Without doubt, language such as this provides significant support for the
contention that a substantial body of late nineteenth-century legal thought
took a somewhat open-ended view of rights-granting state constitutional
provisions. Application of a similar approach to the *federal* Constitution
would, however, be more complex. Depending on one's conception of the
structure of federalism, issues of state-federal relations might counsel
against broad constructions of limitations on state power. Further, even at
the state level the open-ended theory of constitutional interpretation was
somewhat controversial. In *Kamper* itself, John Tyler declared that, in order
for a judge to invalidate a statute, "the [constitutional] violations must be
plain and clear."[34]

Indeed, Roane's own defense of judicial review had originalist overtones.
He argued that "if the legislature may infringe this Constitution, it is no
longer fixed; it is not this year what it was the last; and the liberties of the
people are wholly at the mercy of the legislature."[35] The idea of a Constitution whose meaning was fixed by the original understanding was also supported by other strands of late eighteenth-century thought. In this context,
the need for supplementary rules becomes particularly apparent.

ORIGINALISM AND RELATED THEORIES

Many commentators accept the theory that the framers viewed the original
understanding of some contemporary group as central to the process of constitutional interpretation. The standard originalist account relies on the understanding of the drafters of the Constitution. Others claim that under the
prevailing theories of interpretation in 1789, the appropriate point of reference should be the understanding of the Constitution's ratifiers[36] or the
"common understanding" of the people as a whole.[37] Such assertions are often presented as if they somehow undermine the basic tenets of originalism.
Closer examination, however, reveals that these arguments do not address
the major differences that divide originalism from other strategies of constitutional interpretation.

The primary distinction between originalism and other theories lies in
their perceptions of the mutability of constitutional meaning. Originalists
view the meaning of the Constitution as having been fixed in 1789, while ad-

herents to other interpretive strategies see it as open-ended. From this perspective, it makes little difference if the body with authority to fix the original understanding is the drafters, the ratifiers, or the people as a whole; the
key point is that once settled—by whatever body—it would not evolve over
time as circumstances change.

Moreover, a shift from an examination of the views of the drafters to
those of the ratifiers or the public at large will rarely alter the analysis of specific issues. Both drafters and ratifiers were drawn from the same ruling class
and can be expected to have used language similarly. Moreover, both groups
would presumably have followed common usage in drafting and considering
a constitution—particularly if they believed that the common understanding
would be the benchmark for judicial interpretation. Thus the change in the
corporate source of authority would have little impact on judicial doctrine—
although it might exacerbate some of the practical problems normally associated with originalist methodology. In particular, it would undermine the
canonical significance of the records of the debates at the Philadelphia convention and increase the difficulties involved in interpreting the historical
record generally. Therefore, the need to identify appropriate supplemental
rules of evidence becomes especially critical.

One such set of rules that was well known to the framers can be drawn
from *Blackstone's Commentaries*. While written constitutions as such were
unknown to Blackstone, he did formulate a comprehensive set of maxims to
deal with the problem of statutory interpretation—a process that, according
to many historians, the framers viewed as analogous to constitutional analysis. Blackstone asserted that "the fairest and most rational method to interpret the will of the legislator is by exploring his intentions at the time when
the law was made." Yet he did not advocate a direct inquiry into the subjective understanding of the lawmaking body; instead, he proposed a number
of more or less objective "signs" from which legislative intention was to be
derived. Blackstone began with the principle that "words are generally to be
understood in their usual and most known significance." If the words were
ambiguous, then the judge should have reference to the context, with particular emphasis on the subject matter of the statute. Moreover, if a literal
reading of the statute gave the words "none, or a very absurd signification,"
then the judge "must a little deviate from the received sense of them." In
such a case, Blackstone urged the judge to be guided by "the *reason* and
spirit of [the law]; or the cause which moved the legislator to enact it."[38]

Whatever the influence of Blackstone's maxims during the framing of the
Constitution, they do not adequately answer the need for supplemental evi-

dentiary rules. Such rules come into play only when the constitutional language is unclear on its face; in those cases, Blackstone's precepts are as ambiguous and nonspecific as an unadorned appeal to the original understanding itself. Thus, if the problems besetting originalism are to be resolved, some other plausible source of supplemental rules must be discovered.

Another line of thought that became prominent during the founding era gave more specific guidance to the task of constitutional interpretation. Soon after the Constitution was adopted, state sovereignty theorists developed a new set of supplemental rules that they claimed reflected the original understanding. St. George Tucker, a leading proponent of state sovereignty analysis, provided a succinct encapsulation of his approach to constitutional interpretation:

> Whether [the Constitution] be considered as merely federal, or social, and national, it is that instrument by which *power is created*, on the one hand, and *obedience exacted* on the other. As federal it is to be construed strictly, in all cases where the antecedent rights of a *state* may be drawn in question; as a social compact it ought likewise to receive the same strict construction, wherever the right of personal liberty, of personal security, or of private property may become the subject of dispute; because every person whose liberty or property was thereby rendered subject to the new government, was antecedently a member of a [state] to whose regulations he had submitted himself, and under whose authority and protection he still remains, in all cases not expressly submitted to the new government. The few particular cases in which he submits himself to the new authority, therefore, ought not to be extended beyond the terms of the compact, as it might endanger his obedience to those laws he still continues to owe obedience; or may subject him to a double loss, or inconvenience for the same cause.[39]

Tucker's reasoning would in many circumstances support a substantial measure of judicial interventionism. It would most clearly buttress judicial efforts to establish strict limitations on the powers of Congress, as well as to protect the interests of individual citizens against incursions by the *federal* government. At the same time, however, adoption of Tucker's theory would undermine efforts to wield the Constitution in favor of wide-ranging federal judicial interventionism against *state* government actions. Interventionism in this context would in effect use an instrumentality of the federal government to restrict "the antecedent rights of a *state*"—a practice that was anathema to advocates of state sovereignty.

In any event, state sovereignty analysis cannot be regarded as the definitive expression of the framers' interpretive intent that should guide modern constitutional analysis. First, Tucker's theories were controversial even in the late eighteenth and early nineteenth centuries. James Wilson, for example, rejected the view that the Constitution was either an agreement among states or a social compact; he argued instead that the adoption of the Constitution was an exercise of the primal power of the people and that state governments were necessarily subordinate to that power. Such an approach could easily lead to a far different mode of constitutional interpretation.

Further, even if it had been the dominant theory of 1787, the state sovereignty analysis cannot provide an appropriate framework for a modern approach to constitutional interpretation. The concept of state sovereignty later furnished the theoretical underpinnings for the secessionist position in the Civil War. The victory of the Union armies and subsequent adoption of the Reconstruction amendments represented a clear repudiation of Confederate constitutional opinion. Thus, whatever its historical significance, the concept of state sovereignty should not be the touchstone for the supplemental evidentiary rules necessary to originalist theory.

In short, efforts to identify the interpretive intent of the framers disclose no single dominant approach. Instead, the framers seem to have had a variety of interpretive strategies, some of which were only incompletely articulated, and none of which could claim clear preeminence. Given the historical context in which the Constitution was adopted, the absence of a consensus on this issue should not be surprising. At the time the Constitution was drafted and ratified, both the basic concept of a binding, written constitution and the idea of divided sovereignty that was woven into the Constitution were quite novel. Efforts to develop theories of constitutional interpretation were thus in their infancy and (much like modern debates over theories of judicial review) were complicated by political conflicts. In such an atmosphere, continuing divisions over the proper interpretive strategy were almost inevitable.

Despite their differences, all of the late eighteenth-century approaches to interpretation did agree on one critical point—that the framers of the Constitution had legitimate authority to create binding legal rules. A system of supplemental rules derived from this premise would therefore not only be theoretically sound but could also lay claim to a strong historical pedigree. However, in order to grasp the relationship between the premise of legitimate authority and originalist theory generally, the *source* of the framers' authority must be more closely examined.

CONSTITUTIONAL LEGITIMACY AND THE AUTHORITY OF THE CONSTITUTIONAL CONVENTION

One possible basis for the legitimacy of the Constitution might be the legitimate authority of the Constitutional Convention that drafted the document. Such arguments rest on two premises. First, the convention must have had a mandate to draft an entirely new constitution. Second, the convention must have been authorized to give the new constitution the force of law. The first claim is questionable; the second, entirely indefensible.

The legal authority of the convention derives from a resolution of the national congress established by the Articles of Confederation. The resolution stated that the convention should be held "for the sole and express purpose of revising the articles of Confederation and reporting to Congress and the several state legislatures such alterations and provisions therein as shall, when agreed to in Congress and confirmed by the States, render the federal Constitution adequate to the exigencies of government and preservation of the Union."[40] Two critical points emerge from this resolution. First, the charge was not to produce a completely new constitution but only "alterations and [new] provisions" of the existing Articles of Confederation. More important, the convention was granted no independent authority to enact changes into law; it could merely *recommend* changes that would take effect only after endorsement by other preexisting governmental bodies.

This second point is reemphasized in the Constitution itself; it expressly provides that the new legal regime should take effect only after it had been approved by conventions in at least nine states. The centrality of ratification is further reinforced by Madison's defense of the procedure by which the Constitution was drafted in *Federalist No. 40*. While arguing that the convention had not exceeded its instructions, Madison went on to emphasize that the powers of the convention "were merely advisory and recommendatory" and that any defects in the drafting process were cured by the ratification process.[41] In short, it was the ratification of the Constitution, rather than its drafting, that gave the document legal effect. Therefore, the legitimacy of the document turns on the legitimacy of ratification.

CONSTITUTIONAL LEGITIMACY
AND DEMOCRATIC THEORY

To a large extent, the drafters of the Constitution rested the legitimacy of the ratification process on democratic theory—in the words of Gordon S. Wood, on "the primal power of the people."[42] Madison, for example, contended that "the assent and ratification [is] derived from the supreme authority in each State—the authority of the people themselves."[43] Hamilton's classic argument in favor of judicial review in *Federalist No. 78* is based even more directly on democratic theory: "Where the will of the legislature, declared in its statutes, stands in opposition to that of the people, declared in the Constitution, the judges ought to be governed by the latter rather than the former."[44]

One problem with Hamilton's statement is that it assumes that the will of "the people" does not change over time. The drafting and ratifying conventions might conceivably have reflected the sense of the people in 1787 more accurately than did the legislatures in 1787. One cannot plausibly claim, however, that the delegates to the 1787 and 1788 conventions were more in tune with the ideas of the 1990 populace than officials elected in 1990. Thus, if the federal courts are to be concerned only with carrying out the will of the people, then they should follow more recently adopted statutes instead of the Constitution itself.

The appeal to democratic theory also faces another fundamental obstacle: by modern standards at least, Madison and Hamilton's definition of "the people" is quite narrow. Delegates to the ratification conventions were not selected under a uniform, national code of voter qualifications. Instead, each state set the standards for its own convention; moreover, while the percentage of inhabitants allowed to vote varied widely from state to state, no state government adopted a system remotely resembling the principle of one person, one vote. Slaves were completely excluded; women and free blacks, generally so. Property qualifications were also common. From the perspective of democratic theory, it is difficult to see why the policy preferences of this smaller group of voters in the late 1780s should be seen as having legitimate authority over those of the larger groups that typically vote in modern elections.[45]

Given these problems, the legitimacy of the Constitution (and so the question of judicial review) cannot be defended in terms of democratic theory. Instead, it must rest on some other feature of the Constitution-making process.

CONSTITUTIONAL LEGITIMACY AND
THE POWER OF STATE GOVERNMENTS

A more persuasive explanation sees the source of the Constitution's authority not in the approval of the people but rather in a grant from the state governments in their corporate capacities. After the revolutionary war, sovereign authority passed to the thirteen separate governments controlling the respective territories that comprised the former colonies. The proposed constitution of 1787 called upon those governments to pass a portion of that power to a new, national government. There was, however, a stipulation to this passage of power; each state would retain all preexisting authority unless and until the document was ratified by a convention representing that state (and unless and until eight other states ratified in like manner). By calling ratification conventions and prescribing the form of those conventions, each state government in effect set the conditions under which it would agree to surrender the relevant portion of its power. Since all the conventions ratified the new proposal, the conditions were satisfied in each state, and legitimate authority was conferred on the new national government.

This argument for constitutional legitimacy clearly implies that the Constitution is best conceptualized as a compact among the states. Powell suggests that this conception is fundamentally inconsistent with that of the framers themselves.[46] Admittedly, some federalists such as James Wilson adamantly denied that there was "the least trace of compact in [the] system."[47] In *The Federalist Papers*, however, Madison described the Constitution as an agreement among "distinct and independent States" and called the ratification process "not . . . a *national* but a *federal* act."[48] The difference is that he viewed the process as an act of the *people* of each state, acting together within that state. As we have already seen, this vision is indefensible; the ratification process was controlled not by the people, but by the preexisting state governments. In either case, one central point emerges: the source of authority for the Constitution was not direct agreement given by the people of the United States but rather agreement among the states as discrete, separate entities.[49]

At first glance, this account of the source of constitutional legitimacy might seem to be a simple restatement of the discredited theory of state sovereignty. Certainly, a state compact–based concept of constitutional legitimacy shares some important premises with state sovereignty analysis, but the similarities should not be overstated. The key to the Confederate position was that the states were *exclusively* sovereign—that the federal government exercised authority only as an "agent" of the states. A number of compelling corollaries followed. First, the rights of a citizen in the commonly held territories (including the right to hold slaves) were a function of the law of the citizen's home state. Second, each state possessed authority to determine if a given federal action was constitutional and to secede from the Union if the federal government persisted in unconstitutional action. Finally, the allegiance that a citizen owed to the United States was due only by virtue of the relationship of his state government to the federal authority, and the state government could therefore absolve the citizen from that allegiance.[50]

These elements of state sovereignty theory have one important characteristic in common. They focus on the respective status of the state and federal governments *after* the Constitution was adopted, maintaining that sovereignty remained solely in the states and that the federal government acted only as their agent. By contrast, the vitality of the state compact theory of constitutional legitimacy depends only on two premises: that the state governments possessed sovereign power *before* the drafting and ratification of the Constitution and that they had legitimate authority to surrender a portion of that sovereignty by agreement—an agreement that was manifested by the act of voluntarily participating in the ratification process. The question of the pre-Constitutional status of the states was not at issue during the sectional debates. Instead, the crucial constitutional point dividing the Union and the Confederacy was the relationship between the states and the federal government *after* ratification—in other words, the nature of the compact itself.

Of course, there are other possible objections to the state-centered vision of the legitimacy of the Constitution. For example, it could be contended that the state governments themselves never possessed legitimate sovereign authority and thus could not pass such authority to the federal government. Alternatively, it could be argued that before the drafting of the Constitution, the states were already bound by their voluntary agreement to the Articles of Confederation; that the articles themselves provided a specific mechanism for changing the agreement; that this mechanism could not be circumvented even by unanimous consent; and that the process by which the Constitution was drafted and ratified clearly failed to meet the standards set forth in the articles.[51] As already noted, these arguments do not provide support for nonoriginalist interventionism; instead, they lead inexorably to the conclusion that no legitimate federal government currently exists in the United States. If one is seeking a source for such legitimacy, the state compact theory is the most plausible solution.

STATE COMPACT THEORY AND
THE SCOPE OF ORIGINALIST ANALYSIS

A theory of legitimacy based on the ratification process and the idea of a compact among states has important implications for the scope of originalist constitutional interpretation. The compact itself defines the terms under which the federal courts and the federal government generally should be granted portions of the states' preexisting authority. The Constitution could be ratified only if nine states agreed to it. Put another way, ratifying states agreed to surrender a portion of their governing authority only if eight other states agreed to surrender the same parts of their authority. But if even one of the necessary nine states did not believe that its ratification meant the surrender of a given part of its power to the federal government, then the essential agreement would be deficient. Thus with respect to the original Constitution, only those understandings shared by the necessary majorities voting to ratify in no less than nine state conventions should serve to define the powers granted to the federal government and/or surrendered by the states. The requirements for amendments are even more strict. With the exception of the never-used convention process, all cases entail the concurrence of supermajorities of both houses of Congress as well as the state legislatures. Thus, only those understandings that attracted all the necessary supermajority concurrences should be considered part of the fundamental law.

This formulation creates obvious practical difficulties for originalists. In order to accurately determine the understandings of the ratifiers, one would have to probe the minds of a large number of historical figures, many of whom are obscure and never spoke or wrote publicly on the issues in question. However, an examination of the historical context in which the original Constitution and critical amendments were adopted yields important insights into the understandings that could *not* have gained the requisite agreement.

First, the ratifying conventions of the late 1780s would not have approved the type of broad-ranging authority that has been exercised by the federal government without interference from the Supreme Court in the post-1937 era. Although the drafters and ratifiers of the Constitution agreed on the need to strengthen national authority, many were also ideologically committed to retaining the maximum degree of state autonomy consistent with the necessary functions of a federal government.[52] Further, even those who might have preferred to centralize all power in the federal government were constrained by the political realities of the situation they faced. No state government (or convention called by such a government) was likely to ratify a document that unduly infringed on preexisting state prerogatives, or that gave the federal government the power to dramatically alter the social or economic system of that state. Indeed, many ratifiers believed that they were adopting a system under which, in Madison's words, "the powers of the several States [would] extend to all the objects which, in the ordinary course of affairs, concern the lives, liberties and properties of the people, and internal order, improvement, and prosperity of the people."[53] Preservation of this principle of state autonomy was one of the major concerns of the men who drafted and ratified the Constitution.

The evidence for a narrow original understanding is particularly strong with respect to the commerce clause—the constitutional provision most often cited as the source of sweeping federal authority. This clause was one of the most widely applauded parts of the new Constitution,[54] supported by many (although certainly not all) leading antifederalists.[55] Furthermore, most objections to the clause were based not on apprehensions that it would grant Congress general power over the economic life of the nation but rather on the specific fear that Congress would pass navigation laws that would be unfavorable to the interests of the southern states.[56] This is hardly the pattern of opinion that one would expect if the commerce power had in fact been understood to have the scope attributed to it by post-1937 jurisprudence.

Second, the Reconstruction amendments do not bear the interpretation placed on them by the Supreme Court since the Warren era. Once again, some who voted on the Fourteenth Amendment might well have preferred to impose extensive restraints on state action. They could not, however, have garnered the necessary support for such a sweeping alteration in the structure of constitutional federalism. As will be shown in detail later, other, more conservative elements—whose backing was crucial to the amendment—were quite concerned with maintaining state prerogatives and thus insisted on limiting constitutional change to narrower, more closely circumscribed restrictions on state action.

In short, a consistent application of the most plausible version of originalism would in essence turn contemporary constitutional jurisprudence on its head. Both the power-granting and rights-creating provisions of the Constitution would be confined to the narrow understanding of the framers.

Federal power would face significant limitations; state governments, by contrast, would enjoy far greater freedom of action. Such a prospect is odious to most contemporary constitutional theorists. Thus, it is not surprising that they have launched vigorous attacks on the limitations that originalism would place on federal power and the restrictions it would impose on the federal courts in constitutional adjudication.

THREE

ORIGINALISM AND LIMITS
ON FEDERAL POWER

THE STATUS OF THE DEBATE

For much of American history, issues of federal power have been at the center of the development of constitutional theory and jurisprudence. *Gibbons v. Ogden*[1] and *McCulloch v. Maryland*,[2] both of which defined congressional authority broadly, were among the most important decisions of the Marshall Court. Conversely, Chief Justice Roger Brooke Taney's narrow vision of the scope of congressional authority over the territories was a prominent aspect of the infamous *Dred Scott* decision.[3]

After the Civil War, the idea that Congress could exercise only the powers enumerated in the Constitution became a critical stumbling block to Reconstruction legislation. Sections one and five of the Fourteenth Amendment had been designed largely to expand the authority of the federal government.[4] However, in decisions such as the *Civil Rights Cases*,[5] the Court gave the Reconstruction amendments a narrow reading, limiting substantially the power of Congress over civil rights issues.

The late nineteenth and early twentieth century saw the Court turn its attention once again to the question of congressional power to regulate the economy. Cases such as *E. C. Knight Co. v. United States*[6] and *Hammer v. Dagenhart*[7] drew a sharp distinction between manufacturing and commerce and held that Congress had authority only to regulate the latter. During the Great Depression, this doctrine was used to strike down a wide variety of New Deal legislation in decisions exemplified by *A. L. A. Schecter Poultry Corp. v. United States*[8] and *Carter v. Carter Coal Co.*[9]

The constitutional revolution of 1937 changed this situation dramatically. From 1937 to 1976, there was little support on the Court for the view that the doctrine of enumerated powers imposed substantial restrictions on congressional action. During that period only one federal statute—a law requiring states to allow eighteen-year-olds to vote—was found to be beyond the authority granted to Congress by the Constitution,[10] and this decision was quickly overturned by constitutional amendment. More recently, however, conservative justices have attempted to reinvigorate the concept of states' rights, arguing that the Tenth Amendment places significant limitations on the power of the federal government.

The first major success of the conservative effort came in *National League of Cities v. Usery.*[11] There, overruling *Maryland v. Wirtz*[12] and *Fry v. United States,*[13] the Court struck down the 1974 amendments to the Fair Labor Standards Act, which subjected state and local governments to the requirements of federal minimum wage legislation. Speaking for the majority, Justice Rehnquist asserted that "it is one thing to recognize the authority of Congress to enact laws regulating individual businesses necessarily subject to the dual sovereignty of the government of the Nation and of the State in which they reside. It is quite another to uphold a similar exercise of congressional authority directed, not to private citizens, but to the States as States."[14] He concluded that the amendments to the act were unconstitutional because they infringed on attributes of state sovereignty protected by the Tenth Amendment.

Like *Wirtz* and *Fry* before it, *Usery* soon proved to be something of an unstable precedent. The case drew four dissents, and one member of the majority—Harry A. Blackmun—filed a brief concurrence suggesting that *Usery* should be interpreted narrowly.[15] The depth of Blackmun's commitment to a limiting construction of *Usery* soon became apparent. In *EEOC v. Wyoming*[16] and *Federal Energy Regulatory Commission [FERC] v. Mississippi,*[17] he joined the four *Usery* dissenters in refusing to extend *Usery* beyond the facts of the case itself. Finally, in 1985, Blackmun provided the fifth vote necessary to overrule *Usery* altogether in *Garcia v. San Antonio Metropolitan Transit Authority,*[18] arguing for the majority that the Court's post-*Usery* experience had demonstrated that the analysis in the case was "not only unworkable, but . . . inconsistent with established principles of federalism."[19]

The conservative setback in *Garcia* was temporary, however. *New York v. United States*[20] revealed that, with the replacement of Brennan and Marshall by David Souter and Clarence Thomas, the balance of power on the Court had swung once more to the side of those who favored an *Usery*-type approach to the Tenth Amendment. In *New York*, with all remaining members of the *Garcia* majority dissenting, the Court struck down a provision of the 1985 Low-Level Radioactive Waste Policy Amendments Act that required states to assume ownership of and liability for radioactive waste if they failed to provide for disposal of such waste under federal timetables. While not expressly overruling *Garcia*, the majority opinion declared that "the Framers explicitly chose a Constitution that confers upon Congress the power to regulate individuals, not States;" moreover, "we have always understood that even where Congress has the authority under the Constitution to pass laws requiring or prohibiting certain acts, it lacks the power to compel States to require or prohibit those acts."[21]

Although liberal commentators have portrayed the *Usery-New York* view of the commerce power in exaggerated, alarmist terms[22] the limitations on federal power that the conservative justices would impose are in fact quite modest. The interventionism about which the liberal critics complain is constrained by its own terms to federal government restrictions of state governmental activity. It has no impact on the far more significant extension of federal power to regulate private activities. Conservatives on the Court have been very faithful to these parameters; with the exception of a single vote by Justice Stewart,[23] none of the justices adhering to the Rehnquist analysis of the *Usery-Garcia* problem has ever concluded that Congress exceeded its commerce clause authority in regulating the economic activities of private parties.

The decision in *FERC* has brought the conservative position into sharp perspective. *FERC* was a challenge to a federal statute that focused on the energy-use policies of local public utilities. The statute allowed FERC to exempt local utilities from some state and local regulations but required the state agencies overseeing these utilities to consider certain other types of regulation. The conservative members of the Court dissented from the judgment upholding the mandatory consideration provision,[24] with Justice O'Connor asserting that the statute "conscript[s] state utility commissions into the national bureaucratic army."[25] At the same time, however, the conservatives joined the section of the majority opinion that reaffirmed federal power to overturn directly state regulations of even the intrastate activities of the utilities—a matter that has historically been left to the states.[26] According to Justice O'Connor, the difference was that the direct federal regulation "merely pre-empts state control of private conduct, rather than regulating the 'States as States.' "[27] Similarly, in *Hodel v. Virginia Surface Mining and Reclamation Association*,[28] the conservative justices agreed unanimously that the commerce clause granted Congress authority to pass the Surface Mining Act,[29] notwithstanding Justice Powell's comment that the statute "mandates an extraordinarily intrusive program of federal regulation and control of land use and land reclamation, activities normally left to state and local governments."[30]

The most conservative members of the Court also recognize that Congress retains substantial authority to influence the actions of the state governments themselves. For example, in *United Transportation Union v. Long Island Railroad Co.*,[31] all members of the *Usery* majority joined in holding that the federal government could constitutionally apply the provisions of the Railway Labor Act to proprietary activities of state and local governments. Similarly, in *New York*, the majority agreed that although Congress could not force states to enact legislation dealing with the problem of nuclear waste, it could provide incentives for such legislation.[32]

In short, even the most interventionist contemporary justices have allowed Congress to exercise authority far beyond that envisioned by the framers of the commerce clause. Seeking to preserve the fruits of the revolution of 1937, some liberal commentators have contended that the commerce clause was originally understood to grant Congress general authority over the economic life of the nation. As I argued in chapter two, this view is insupportable. Cognizant of this difficulty, other supporters of broad congressional power have taken different approaches.

THE REVOLUTION OF 1937
AS LEGITIMATE CONSTITUTIONAL CHANGE

Bruce A. Ackerman contends that the framers themselves would have regarded the expansion of federal authority in 1937 as a legitimate alteration of the Constitution. According to Ackerman, the framers envisioned a Supreme Court that would, on occasion, act as the agent of the people as a whole in identifying and implementing constitutional changes that the people had "adopted" in a manner other than that outlined in Article V— what he describes as "irregular" constitutional politics. He argues that the 1937 shift was an example of such irregular constitutionmaking.[33] As Suzanna Sherry has demonstrated,[34] however, Ackerman's analysis of the historical evidence cannot withstand serious scrutiny.

At the outset, it should be clear that Ackerman bears a heavy burden in defending his thesis. The Constitution was a carefully crafted set of compromises among various principles and interests. It includes two detailed amendment procedures that were an integral part of that compromising. Under normal circumstances, one would therefore expect the Article V procedures to be the exclusive avenue for explicit constitutional change.

Ackerman attempts to deal with this problem by drawing together several themes from *The Federalist Papers*. First, he observes that Publius recognized that the Constitution itself was in some sense illegal, because its ratification would not satisfy the conditions specified in the Articles of Confederation; nonetheless, Publius argued, the adoption of the Constitution would be a legitimate exercise of political power.[35] From this Ackerman infers that the framers believed that alterations in constitutional structure could sometimes be adopted through irregular means.[36]

Next, Ackerman notes that the framers understood that they were constructing a government based on what he describes as a "semiotic" theory of representation, in which the elected representatives would not merely mimic the will of a majority of the people but rather would deliberate and take those actions that were in the best interests of the nation.[37] He connects this point with Publius's repeated references to the supremacy of the people in order to argue that when "we the people" unambiguously express their desire for constitutional change, the Court should respect that wish, even if not expressed through the mechanisms provided in Article V.

In making this claim, Ackerman relies primarily on a long passage from Hamilton's defense of judicial review in *Federalist No. 78*. Hamilton first asserts that the power of judicial review does not

> by any means suppose a superiority of the judicial to the legislative power. It only supposes that the power of the people is superior to both, and that where the will of the legislature, declared in its statutes, stands in opposition to that of the people, declared in the Constitution, the judges ought to be governed by the latter rather than the former.[38]

After noting the power of the people to change the Constitution, Hamilton continues:

> Yet it is not to be inferred from this principle that the representatives of the people, whenever a momentary inclination happens to lay hold of a majority of their constituents incompatible with the provisions of the existing constitution, would, on that account, be justifiable in a violation of those provisions; or that the courts would be under a greater obligation to connive at infractions in this shape than when they had proceeded wholly from the cabals of the representative body. Until the people by some solemn and authoritative act, annulled or changed the established form, it is binding upon themselves collectively, as well as individually; and no presumption, or even knowledge of their sentiments, can warrant their representatives in a departure from it prior to such an act. But it is easy to see that it would require an uncommon portion of fortitude to do their duty as faithful guardians of the Consti-

tution, where legislative invasions of it had been instigated by the major voice of the community.[39]

Ackerman contends that this passage "provides a wonderful summary of all the themes we have rehearsed: Publius's dualistic understanding of the People, his semiotic concept of representation, and his complex analysis interact to yield a distinctive view of the Court's understanding."[40]

The key question, of course, is what constitutes a "solemn and authoritative act" of the people. Given its context, as Sherry observes,[41] the most natural reading of this passage is that it refers specifically and exclusively to the procedure outlined in Article V. Alternatively, it might refer to some other formal action taken by the people to change the Constitution, even where the specific form of action was different from that delineated in Article V. This interpretation would support the arguments of (for example) Akhil R. Amar, who suggests that a national referendum on constitutional change might have the necessary legitimacy.[42] It might also serve to vitiate arguments against the validity of the Fourteenth Amendment, which was adopted through procedures that are somewhat questionable when measured against the strict requirements of Article V and the remainder of the pre-Civil War Constitution.[43]

Ackerman's theory, however, goes considerably beyond Amar's conception. He concedes that during the New Deal, Congress exercised power to a degree far in excess of that contemplated by the framers. He contends, however, that valid constitutional change can sometimes take place even where *no* explicit effort was made to alter the document itself. He argues that the ultimate acceptance of the New Deal was just such an example.[44]

Here Ackerman's historical argument collapses completely. The only events during the 1930s that might plausibly be described as reflecting the voice of "we the people" on the constitutional issues—the passage and reenactment of New Deal legislation, the reelection of Franklin Roosevelt in 1936, and Roosevelt's use of the appointment power to reshape the Court into a more friendly institution—were, in procedural terms, ordinary exercises of authority, explicitly sanctioned in the preexisting Constitution itself. To find legitimate constitutional change in such circumstances is to rely at best on a "presumption or . . . knowledge of [the people's] sentiment" and at worst on "a momentary inclination [that] happens to lay hold of a majority of [the people]" in order to justify otherwise unconstitutional action taken by Congress—the very circumstances that Hamilton argued would *not* validate such action. Thus, Ackerman fails to provide the necessary historical evidence to support his model of irregular constitutional change.

FEDERALISM AND THE STRUCTURE
OF THE POLITICAL PROCESS

Herbert Wechsler and Jesse H. Choper take a different tack in urging the Court to adopt a noninterventionist posture with respect to the doctrine of enumerated powers.[45] They argue that the structure of the political branches offers sufficient protection for states' rights and that judicial review is therefore unnecessary to restrain the power of the federal government in cases where no "individual rights" are involved. Choper even contends that questions of whether Congress has exceeded its enumerated powers should be viewed as entirely nonjusticiable political questions. The majority opinion in *Garcia* relied heavily on this reasoning in overruling *Usery*.[46]

The basic idea that judicial intervention should be limited by "prudential" considerations can find substantial historical backing.[47] For example, in *Marbury v. Madison*, Chief Justice Marshall explicitly recognized that the Court had no authority to adjudicate so-called political questions,[48] and throughout its history the Court has at times turned to this theory to avoid deciding issues that it believes are best left to the other branches. Prudential doctrines such as standing, mootness, and ripeness have also at times provided the justification for judicial restraint.

Limitations on judicial authority can also be inferred directly from the text of the Constitution itself. For example, the Constitution states that each house of Congress is the arbiter of the "Elections, Returns, and Qualifications of its own Members" and clearly divides the power of impeachment and removal of the president and federal judges between the House of Representatives and the Senate. Curtailment of judicial review in such cases fits comfortably within the fundamental tenets of originalist theory.

Despite the strong historical pedigree behind the idea of prudential restraints, the Wechsler/Choper argument faces formidable difficulties. First, the accuracy of the empirical assumptions that underlie their position is questionable at best. Admittedly, the interests of the states qua states are represented to some extent in the national political process. As Laurence H. Tribe has observed, however, "the [simple] fact that Congress is made up of representatives of states does not assure that the legislature will give adequate respect to the rights of states."[49] Indeed, the recent record of Congress speaks volumes to the contrary; while considerations of federalism may have restrained legislative action in some circumstances, cases such as *FERC* and *Hodel* illustrate well the degree to which the federal government has been willing to intrude on both the traditional substantive prerogatives of the states and the structure through which those prerogatives are exercised.[50]

The attempt to differentiate between issues of federalism and questions of individual rights is beset with conceptual problems as well. For example, although the concept of enumerated powers and the Tenth Amendment provided the legal backdrop for the constitutional challenge to the statute in *Hodel*, the right of the state governments to regulate land use as they pleased was not the only issue in the case. For the landowners, what was at stake was their liberty to operate surface mines on their property free from federal interference—plainly an individual right. Similar issues are also inherent in most other suits against federal action.

Thus the doctrine of enumerated powers has two functions, which are often conflated by the commentators.[51] On one hand, the doctrine preserves the prerogatives of the preexisting state governments; on the other, it protects the people generally from government oppression, not by *preserving* the authority of the states, but simply by *limiting* the power of the national government. The framers themselves were clearly aware of this dichotomy. The idea that the doctrine of enumerated powers was a prime source of protection for the rights of the people was specifically noted by Alexander Hamilton in *The Federalist Papers*[52] and by other prominent federalists, such as Oliver Ellsworth of Connecticut, Theophilus Parsons of Massachusetts, and James Wilson of Pennsylvania.[53] Indeed, in the absence of a bill of rights—which, it must be remembered, was added only after ratification—the doctrine of enumerated powers was perhaps the most important guaranty that the federal government would not become oppressively intrusive.

The Tenth Amendment, with its reservation of rights to the people as well as the states, reflects a similar understanding. The amendment is generally ignored or downplayed by most modern nonoriginalist commentators; however, when adopted in the late eighteenth century, it embodied the belief that the doctrine of enumerated powers was one of the most important protections for individual liberty in the new Constitution.[54] Indeed, Samuel Spencer—a prominent antifederalist—expressed the view that a sufficiently strong reaffirmation of that principle "would render a Bill of Rights unnecessary."[55] Others, including Samuel Adams, made comparable assertions.[56]

Moreover, while anxious to create a government with authority to regulate the interstate and international movement of goods, the framers had particular reason to fear a central authority with sweeping power to control all of the economic affairs of the nation. Property rights ranked particularly high in the framers' pantheon,[57] and their experience with the state governments demonstrated that unrestricted governmental power posed a great danger to those rights.[58] An overly powerful national government would only magnify the possibility that legislation would infringe unduly on the sacred rights of property.

Further, although Madison did argue that the structure of the new system would help preserve both the autonomy of the states and the rights of the people,[59] Hamilton's defense of judicial review in *The Federalist Papers* applies to the doctrine of enumerated powers as well as to provisions specifically defining individual rights. Hamilton's argument is that the Constitution is law; because it is to be ratified by a higher authority, it supersedes and invalidates contrary rules promulgated by the ordinary legislative process.[60] Congressional action not authorized by the enumerated powers described in the Constitution violates the express provisions of the Tenth Amendment. Hamilton's analysis thus compels the conclusion that the Court should not defer to the judgment of Congress in such cases but should find the action unconstitutional. Ellsworth was more specific, asserting that "if the United States go beyond their powers, if they make a law which the Constitution does not authorize, it is void; and the judicial power, the national judges, who, to secure their impartiality, are to be made independent, will declare it to be void."[61]

In short, neither the courts nor the commentators have given an adequate justification for treating individual rights cases differently from those dealing with the issue of enumerated powers. Most of the modern nonoriginalist literature, however, has not focused on the argument that originalism leads the Court to an unduly interventionist position. Instead, it has sought to justify greater judicial interventionism than would be mandated by the original understanding.

FOUR
DEMOCRATIC THEORY, LEGITIMACY, AND NONORIGINALIST INTERVENTIONISM

Analysis of the case for nonoriginalist interventionism starts with the theory of pure politics. As already noted, federal judges are in a position to shape public policy by invoking the Constitution. Interventionists begin by asking why the judges should limit themselves to the original understanding in exercising this power rather than seek more generally to better the law. Noninterventionists have typically made two different arguments in response: the argument from democratic theory, and the argument from legitimacy.

DEMOCRATIC THEORY AND NONORIGINALIST INTERVENTIONISM

Attacks on nonoriginalist interventionism have most often centered on the relationship between judicial review and democratic theory. Noninterventionists have been quick to contend that interventionism is fundamentally inconsistent with a political system based on the premise of majoritarian decisionmaking. In a 1976 article, Chief Justice William Rehnquist captured the essence of this argument:

> To the extent that it makes possible an individual's persuading one or more appointed federal judges to impose on other individuals a rule of conduct that the popularly elected branches of government would not have enacted and the voters have not and would not have embodied in the Constitution, [nonoriginalist interventionist theory] is genuinely corrosive of the fundamental values of our democratic society.[1]

Interventionists have generally taken the view that the so-called countermajoritarian difficulty is the primary theoretical obstacle to an interventionist approach.[2] As John Hart Ely has noted, in American society the charge that a particular methodology is antidemocratic has considerable sentimental force.[3] Nonetheless, the appeal to democratic theory faces substantial difficulties.

First, the suggestion that interventionist judicial review is invariably antimajoritarian is based on an oversimplified model of the place of judicial review in the political process. According to this view, constitutional interventionism inevitably displaces the judgments of the representative branches of government (generally, the legislature) with those of an unelected judiciary. Although many so-called individual rights cases fit well into this model, the relationship between interventionism and the governmental decisionmaking process is often more complex.

At times, the Court will not simply be faced with the decision of a single popularly elected body; instead, it will be allocating power between two such bodies. Consider, for example, *National League of Cities v. Usery*,[4] in which the Court struck down a congressional statute that imposed minimum wage requirements on the institutions of state government. In its decision, the Court voided a policy judgment of Congress, a popularly elected body of government; at the same time, it revivified the power of other democratically chosen officials—those representing state and local governments. Thus, a persuasive critique of *Usery* (and so of interventionism) cannot rest on the theory of majoritarian government.

Similar ambiguities can be found in some individual rights cases as well. The clearest examples arise when the federal courts are reviewing not legislative actions but state *judicial* decisions. In these situations, an interventionist approach can sometimes be consistent with democratic theory, even where the structure of the political process is not directly implicated. The Court's treatment of *Pruneyard Shopping Center v. Robins*[5] dramatically illustrates this point.

Pruneyard was the last in a series of decisions in which the Court dealt with the federal constitutional problems involved in attempts by private parties to use private shopping centers to express views on matters of public interest. Initially, in *Food Employees Local 590 v. Logan Valley Plaza, Inc.,*[6] the Court held that shopping centers were analogous to "company towns"; thus, the First and Fourteenth amendments prevented the owners of shopping centers from prohibiting expressive conduct.[7] The *Logan Valley* doctrine was short-lived, however; the holding in the case was sharply limited in *Lloyd Corp. v. Tanner*[8] and overruled in *Hudgens v. NLRB*.[9] Thus when *Pruneyard* came to the Court, federal constitutional law clearly did not require shopping-center owners to open the malls to political discussion.

In *Pruneyard*, the Court was presented with the flip side of the *Logan Valley* coin. The California Supreme Court had held that the state constitution required shopping centers to allow the use of their facilities for discussion of public issues.[10] The owners of a shopping center argued that this ruling violated their First Amendment rights and constituted a taking of private property without compensation. The Supreme Court unanimously rejected these arguments, applying a deferential standard of review and concluding that the California rule was not " 'unreasonable, arbitrary, or capricious.' "[11]

The Court's decision to defer cannot have reflected a belief in the general superiority of legislative decisionmaking. The reason is quite simple: no legislative judgment was involved in *Pruneyard*. Instead, the challenged rule was a state *judicial* gloss on the state constitution. Indeed, if legislative autonomy had been the central issue, the Court should have scrutinized the California Supreme Court judgment closely; by holding that the state constitution required shopping-center owners to allow political speech, the state court had removed the subject from normal legislative consideration. Thus, had the Court used an interventionist analysis in *Pruneyard*, it would have vindicated the principle of majoritarian rule.

Cases like *Usery* and *Pruneyard* demonstrate the inadequacy of the model of judicial review that undergirds the focus on democratic theory. Moreover, as Ely points out, even where the Court is reviewing legislative judgments, interventionism can at times be consistent with or even demanded by democratic theory. The most obvious examples are cases dealing with voting rights. At the very least, democratic principles require that all citizens have the right to vote and that each citizen's vote counts equally. Before the 1960s, the electoral process and governmental organization of many states was inconsistent with this axiom. Only dramatic action by the Warren Court brought the states more closely into line with the one person, one vote principle. For example, *Reynolds v. Sims*[12] and its progeny established the rule that legislative elections should be governed by the formula of one person, one vote, and cases such as *Harper v. Virginia Board of Elections*[13] expanded access to the franchise. In these situations, democratic theory and judicial interventionism were partners; interventionism became the vehicle by which the basic theory of majoritarian rule was implemented.

In short, not all nonoriginalist interventionism is inconsistent with even the narrowest definition of democratic theory. Moreover, even where the Court is clearly thwarting the will of the majority, the appeal to democracy is an inadequate response to interventionist arguments. As many interventionist theorists have pointed out, most Americans would consider *some* values more important than the preservation of majoritarian decisionmaking. Indeed, the text of the Constitution itself recognizes this point by explicitly limiting the powers of both the state and national legislatures. Thus, in its pure form the appeal to democratic theory would condemn not only nonoriginalist approaches but also originalist interventionism. Originalists must therefore deploy some other argument if the two philosophies are to be successfully differentiated.

LEGITIMACY AND NONORIGINALIST INTERVENTIONISM

Commentators who attack the theoretical foundations of nonoriginalist review also argue that it lacks "legitimacy."[14] Robert H. Bork has provided the most complete defense of this postulate.[15] Bork ties legitimacy in constitutional adjudication to the concept of "neutral principles" championed by Herbert Wechsler[16] and R. Kent Greenawalt.[17] Wechsler argues that "a principled decision . . . is one that rests on reasons with respect to all issues in the case, reasons that in their generality and their neutrality transcend any immediate result that is involved."[18] Bork extends this argument, asserting that the principles controlling constitutional interventionism must be neutral not only in *application* but also in *definition* and *derivation*. He concludes that only a jurisprudence based on the original understanding satisfies these criteria.

Bork's argument has a powerful emotional pull. The ideology of neutral principles is deeply rooted in the American political psyche, and the overt lack of neutrality in nonoriginalist interventionism is a source of considerable unease to many noninterventionist theorists. Nonoriginalists have adopted a variety of different approaches in attempting to deal with this problem. These approaches typically fall into two classes: neo-originalist and functional.

FIVE

NEO-ORIGINALIST DEFENSES
OF JUDICIAL INTERVENTIONISM

Many scholars adopt what might be described as neo-originalist strategies to defend judicial interventionism. While seeking to clothe their theories with the authority of the original understanding, these commentators claim that the original understanding allows or even demands that the judiciary adopt an open-ended approach to the definition of constitutional rights. By adopting this strategy, neo-originalists seek to avoid problems of legitimacy.

RELIANCE ON SPECIFIC CLAUSES

The most popular neo-originalist defense of judicial interventionism contends that specific clauses in the Constitution by their nature invite such interventionism. Any number of constitutional provisions have been cited as authority for this position; Richard A. Epstein, for example, relies on the takings clause[1] and the contracts clause[2] to support wide-ranging protection for economic liberty, while Harold M. Hyman and William M. Wiecek[3] argue for a broad interpretation of the Thirteenth Amendment. The most widely-cited candidates, however, are the Ninth Amendment and section one of the Fourteenth Amendment.

The Ninth Amendment[4]

For most of American history, the Ninth Amendment played little part in discussions of theories of constitutional interpretation. Since Justice Goldberg's reference to the amendment in *Griswold v. Connecticut*,[5] however, it has become an important weapon in the interventionist arsenal. Commentators as diverse as Randy E. Barnett,[6] John Hart Ely,[7] Leonard Levy,[8] and Laurence H. Tribe and Michael C. Dorf[9] have turned to the amendment as full or partial justification for their interventionist theories.

Unlike the first eight amendments, the Ninth Amendment does not protect specific rights. Instead, it provides that "the enumeration in the Constitution, of certain rights, shall not be construed to deny or disparage others retained by the people." The debate over the original understanding of the amendment has focused on the question of whether the framers believed that courts should rely on unenumerated rights to overturn otherwise invulnerable legislative action. Sharply differing views have emerged over this issue.

Raoul Berger,[10] Russell Caplan,[11] Thomas B. McAffee,[12] and James Hutson[13] have furnished the most extensive defenses of the narrow view of the amendment. These four scholars argue that the framers intended only to guard a wide range of state-created rights from the suggestion that they were somehow eliminated by the enumeration of rights in the federal Constitution. They contend, however, that the amendment was not understood to guarantee that these rights would not be invaded by extraconstitutional government action. Obviously, under this interpretation, the Ninth Amendment does not provide a justification for neooriginalist interventionism.

Other writers take a much more expansive view of the original understanding of the Ninth Amendment. Drawing on the work of scholars such as Thomas Grey and Suzanna Sherry,[14] the proponents of the expansive interpretation first note that the framers were operating against the background of a legal culture that recognized the existence of judicially enforceable natural rights. They reason that the Ninth Amendment was intended to protect this natural law tradition from the potential implication that it was inconsistent with and invalidated by the listing of specific rights in a written constitution.

Resolution of the dispute over the original understanding of the Ninth Amendment requires consideration of a number of different issues. The first is the place of natural law in the jurisprudence of the late eighteenth century. On this point, defenders of an expansive reading of the Ninth Amendment are on solid ground. Most of the framers clearly did believe in natural law—at least in the abstract. The question of the relationship of natural law to positive law, however, remained controversial during the founding era.[15]

The well-known decision in *Calder v. Bull*[16] illustrates the essence of the controversy. *Calder* involved a dispute over the right to inherit from the estate of a Dr. Morrison. The Bulls claimed that the will of Dr. Morrison's grandson established their right to inherit; the Calders relied on the law of intestate succession. After the Connecticut probate court initially ruled in favor of the Calders, the legislature approved a statute granting the Bulls a new hearing, at which the Bulls prevailed. The Calders argued that the state action violated the state constitution, the federal constitutional prohibition on *ex post facto* laws, and basic principles of natural law.

While all members of the Supreme Court agreed that the Calders' claim should be rejected, the opinions in the case revealed widely divergent views on the role of natural law in judicial decisionmaking. Samuel Chase argued vigorously for judicial enforcement of natural law:

> I cannot subscribe to the omnipotence of a state Legislature, or that it is absolute and without control, although its authority should not be expressly restrained by the constitution, or fundamental law, of the state. . . . There are certain vital principles in our free Republican governments, which will determine and overrule an apparent and flagrant abuse of legislative power; as to authorize manifest injustice by positive law; or take away that security for personal liberty, or personal property, for protection whereof government was established. An act of the Legislature (for I cannot call it a law) contrary to the first principle of the social compact, cannot be considered a rightful exercise of legislative authority.[17]

By contrast, William Paterson and James Iredell expressed a quite different perspective on the relationship between natural law and positive law. Paterson opined that retrospective laws generally "accord with [neither] sound legislation, nor the fundamental principles of the social compact." Nonetheless, he felt constrained to uphold the Connecticut statute because it did not fall within the technical meaning of the term *"ex post facto* laws."[18] The juxtaposition of these two views clearly implies that Paterson regarded positive law as superior to the "fundamental principles of the social compact." Iredell was even more explicit in his assertion of the supremacy of positive law, declaring that "if . . . the legislature of the union, or the legislature of any member of the union, shall pass a law, within the general scope of their constitutional power, the court cannot pronounce it void, merely because it is, in their judgment, contrary to the principles of natural law."[19]

Calder indicates that there was a distinct division of opinion over the relationship between natural law and positive law during the founding period. Thus, given the premise that, in doubtful cases, the original understanding should generally be interpreted narrowly, the open-ended view of the Ninth Amendment must be rejected. However, even assuming that Chase's position characterized the framers' views, advocates of the open-ended theory would still confront other problems.

First, even if the amendment was understood to constitutionalize some unenumerated rights, there is no indication that the rights so protected would change over time. The language of the amendment is at least as consistent with the perception that it secured a *fixed* class of rights.[20] Moreover, this view fits comfortably with the historical context in which the Bill of Rights was adopted. The driving force behind the amendments was not the idea that the Supreme Court should take a leading role in the evolution of new concepts of societal values; indeed, many of the most vociferous advocates of a bill of rights feared federal judicial "creativity" as much as congressional power. Instead, the proposed amendments were meant to ensure that the new federal government *as a whole* would not invade certain rights that were widely regarded as fundamental at the time. A Ninth Amendment that protected a fixed set of rights is more consistent with this purpose than one whose parameters would change over time.

This line of reasoning would make the Ninth Amendment susceptible to interpretation by the same approach to historical analysis that undergirds standard originalist theory. Of course, some of the conclusions drawn from such analysis might well be controversial, particularly at the margins. Thus, for example, there might be some dispute over the extent to which the Ninth Amendment prevented government from imposing stringent regulations on the use of private property. At the very least, however, one should be able to conclude reliably that a wide range of rights were understood *not* to be protected by the Ninth Amendment.

One prominent example is the kind of strong, unenumerated *political* rights that form the basis of Ely's representation-reinforcement theory of constitutional adjudication. The constitutional text itself deals specifically with these issues. Guidelines for the right to vote in federal elections and to hold federal office are spelled out in great detail, while the forms of state government are limited only by the admonition that they be "republican"—a requirement that, given the historical milieu, left the states great leeway. Since these political rights *are* enumerated in the Constitution, they cannot plausibly be viewed as having been within the scope of the Ninth Amendment's reference to "rights retained by the people." Thus the Ninth Amendment cannot be used to justify Ely's approach.

Even more important, the mere fact that the Ninth Amendment acknowledged the existence of fundamental, unenumerated rights does not imply that it constitutionalized such rights. To appreciate the significance of this point, one must begin with an examination of the precise claim advanced by commentators who take the expansive view. They cannot effectively argue that Ninth Amendment rights were created by the Constitution itself; indeed, the crux of their position is that the amendment protects some rights not established by the written document. Consequently, their argument must be that the rights whose existence is recognized by the Ninth Amendment should be viewed as part of an "unwritten" or "common law" constitution, different from and supplementary to its written counterpart.

Here a statutory analogy is instructive. Federal statutes commonly contain "nonpreemption" provisions, specifying that preexisting state law dealing with the same subject as the statute should remain intact unless fundamentally inconsistent with the statute. In such cases, the enacting Congress no doubt acts against a background understanding of the existing state law and may well pass the federal statute in the belief that the state law will not essentially change. But no one would suggest that the federal statute is the source of authority for the rights left unaffected by the nonpreemption provision; instead, those rights derived their authority from the actions of the enacting states, which remain free to modify or even abrogate them as they see fit. The statement of nonpreemption simply declares that the states will retain the same freedom in this respect that they possessed before the passage of the statute.

The Ninth Amendment is phrased in similar nonpreemption language. Considered from this angle, even under the most expansive view of the framers' attitude toward natural law, the unenumerated rights recognized by the amendment would not rise to the level of written constitutional norms. The framers of the amendment did not create those rights through the operation of the legitimate constitutionmaking process envisioned by originalists; at most, the framers simply *assumed* that a body of rights existed prior to the making of the written constitution and resolved that the adoption of written constraints on government should not destroy those preexisting, extratextual rights. But by definition, the body of rights protected by the Ninth Amendment is not constitutional at all, but rather extraconstitutional. Since the recognized rights are not created by the legitimate functioning of the constitutionmaking process, the Constitution cannot be seen as mandating their protection.

Under this reading, the Ninth Amendment would not be perceived as a requirement that the judiciary discover and protect extratextual fundamental rights. Instead, it would simply remove a bar to interventionism that is beyond the scope of the original understanding—a bar that might otherwise be found to be implicit in the grant of powers to Congress and the reservation of rights to the states in the Tenth Amendment. Advocates of such interventionism would still have to resolve the problem of constructing a persuasive functional or theoretical justification for their position.

Finally, even if these other difficulties could be surmounted, the Ninth Amendment would not support federal judicial interventionism aimed at the actions of state governments. Commentators on the Ninth Amendment typically concede that the amendment was initially understood to be only a constraint on the federal government.[21] The idea that the Ninth Amendment should be considered in describing restraints on state governments depends largely on acceptance of the controversial thesis that section one of the Fourteenth Amendment was intended to make the Bill of Rights applicable to the states.[22] Once this premise is accepted, Ninth Amendment *aficionados* argue that to exclude the Ninth Amendment from the incorporation doctrine can only be viewed as a manifestation of the intellectually unpalatable concept of "selective incorporation."[23]

The trouble with this argument is that it rests on an ahistorical definition of the phrase "Bill of Rights." In modern parlance, "Bill of Rights" does refer to the first ten amendments to the Constitution. During the Reconstruction era, however, the reach of the phrase seems to have been somewhat more limited. Cong. John A. Bingham of Ohio and Sen. Jacob Howard of Michigan—the two authorities relied on most heavily by defenders of the incorporation theory—stated that section one incorporated the first *eight* amendments.[24] Thus the historical record of the incorporation theory would not support the application of the Ninth Amendment to the states.

In short, even if one assumes that the Ninth Amendment embodied the framers' belief in nontextual rights that were judicially enforceable, it provides at best a shaky foundation for a theory of neo-originalist interventionism. It is not surprising, therefore, that advocates of such a theory more often rely on the Fourteenth Amendment to justify their position.

The Fourteenth Amendment

The Fourteenth Amendment is the most popular source for the claim that the original understanding of the Constitution itself mandates open-ended interventionism. On its face, the language of section one of the amendment—particularly the privileges and immunities and equal protection clauses—seems to be an unqualified invitation to the courts to constitutionalize their own conceptions of fundamental rights and equality. For interventionist commentators such as John Hart Ely, Robert A. Sedler, and Laurence H. Tribe, the language is so clear on this point that no detailed examination of the original understanding is necessary.[25]

Tribe's approach to equal protection analysis is typical. He argues that equal protection jurisprudence should be guided by what he describes as the "antisubjugation principle," which would invalidate "conditions [that], examined in their social and historical context, are a manifestation or a legacy of official suppression." Tribe's more general defense of an interventionist judiciary is based largely on functional considerations (to be addressed in the next chapter). At the same time, however, he seeks to invoke the authority of the framers in support of the antisubjugation principle, asserting that the equal protection clause is "more . . . a delphic edict than . . . an intelligible rule of decision"; that "the opacity of the clause cries out for a mediating principle"; and that the antisubjugation principle is "faithful to the historical origins of the Civil War amendments."[26] Yet a quite different picture emerges when section one is placed in the context of Republican political thought and the overall legal culture of the mid-nineteenth century.[27]

From this perspective, the drafters' view of the privileges and immunities clause comes into clear focus. The language of the clause was drawn directly from the privileges and immunities clause of Article IV[28]—the comity clause—which required states to grant many of the same rights to transients that they provided to their own citizens. A substantial body of caselaw interpreting the comity clause existed at the time the Fourteenth Amendment was drafted.[29] These precedents held uniformly that the protections of the comity clause extended only to *fundamental* rights of citizenship. Moreover, the cases consistently listed the same rights as fundamental—generally those that Congress protected by statute in the Civil Rights Act of 1866, although references to the principles of the Bill of Rights also made appearances.[30]

The due process and equal protection clauses also had deep roots in the legal culture of the mid-1860s.[31] The due process clause (or its equivalent, the "law of the land" clause) was included not only in the federal Bill of Rights but also in every state constitution. Such clauses obviously had important procedural implications. In addition, due process analysis was occasionally given a substantive content by state courts. At times it was used to invalidate laws that arbitrarily deprived individuals of vested rights. In other cases, it was the vehicle for attacks on "class legislation"—laws that singled out individuals or (more rarely) small groups for less advantageous treatment than the populace as a whole. Once again, however, its employment in this context was limited to deprivations of vested rights—either natural rights or rights established by statute.

Similarly, in the mid-1800s, the right to protection of the laws was understood not only by Republicans but by all mainstream American political theorists to be a discrete, fundamental interest, related to but different from other important rights.[32] This right—recognized as distinct in the antebellum comity clause cases[33] as well as by distinguished commentators such as

Chancellor James Kent[34] and Francis Lieber[35]—had two major components. The first was the right to protection *from* government—a mostly procedural usage, requiring that government proceed through legal forms when interfering with the rights of the citizenry. The majority opinion in the landmark decision of *Ex parte Milligan*,[36] decided contemporaneously with the drafting of the Fourteenth Amendment, relied eloquently on this concept. Finding that a military tribunal had no jurisdiction to try and convict a civilian in a loyal state, Justice David Davis argued:

> It is the birthright of every American citizen when charged with crime to be tried and punished according to law. The power of punishment is alone the means through which the laws have provided for the purpose and if they are ineffectual, there is an immunity from punishment. . . . By the protection of the law human rights are secured; withdraw that protection and they are at the mercy of wicked rulers, or the clamor of an excited people.[37]

The nineteenth-century rendering of equal protection also included a right to protection *by* government.[38] This component was essentially parasitic. It created no substantive interests itself; instead, it required governmental protection of those interests guaranteed either by natural or positive law.[39]

Taken together, these principles paint a picture of the equal protection clause radically different from the classification-based theories that dominate modern constitutional jurisprudence. They point instead to a model described by Chief Justice Lemuel Shaw of the Supreme Judicial Court of Massachusetts in *Roberts v. City of Boston*. There a Boston ordinance requiring schools to be racially segregated was challenged under a Massachusetts constitutional provision mandating "equality before the law." Rejecting the state constitutional claim, Shaw concluded:

> The great principle . . . is that by the constitution and laws of Massachusetts all persons . . . are equal before the law. This, as a broad general principle . . . is perfectly sound. . . . But when this great principle comes to be applied to the actual and various conditions of persons in society, it will not warrant the assertion, that men and women are legally clothed with the same civil and political powers, and that children and adults are legally to have the same functions and be subject to the same treatment; *but only that the rights of all, as they are settled and regulated by law, are equally entitled to the paternal consideration and*

protection of the law, for their maintenance and security. What those rights are, to which individuals, in the infinite variety of circumstances by which they are surrounded in society, are entitled, must depend on laws adapted to their respective relations and conditions.[40]

The standard analysis of the *Roberts* case describes Sen. Charles Sumner, the attorney for the plaintiff, as a hero whose argument presaged the conceptions of racial equality later embodied in the Fourteenth Amendment, and Shaw as a villain whose retrograde views on the nature of equal protection were to haunt American jurisprudence for one hundred years.[41] This characterization ignores the fact that Shaw was not seeking to *define* "equal protection"; he was simply *using* that concept to describe the import of "equality before the law." Moreover, the structure of Shaw's opinion reflects the dichotomy between the concepts of equality of rights and equality of protection respectively, which appears in antebellum arguments generally. Under this view, all men—black or white—were equally entitled to protection of the laws to enforce their legal rights; but unless a particular interest could be classified as a natural or vested right, the legislature could withhold that interest from any class at will. Since public education was neither a natural nor vested right, the legislature would only have run afoul of basic equal protection principles by taxing blacks to support educational institutions and then denying them access to equal benefits from such institutions.

Despite the relatively limited scope of privileges and immunities, due process, and equal protection in antebellum thought, all three concepts played significant roles in the pre–Civil War debate over slavery. Southerners began with the assertion that slaves were a constitutionally protected species of property. Consequently, as long as their home states recognized the institution of slavery, the privileges and immunities clause guaranteed them the right to bring slaves temporarily into free states without the slaves' being freed by state law. They further contended that efforts to outlaw slavery in the District of Columbia and the federally held territories deprived them of their property without due process of law.

The concept of equal protection of the law figured even more prominently in the proslavery arguments. The defenders of slavery claimed that refusal to take positive action establishing slavery in the territories denied them equal protection of the law for their property rights.[42] On the eve of the Civil War, Sen. Robert A. Toombs of Georgia went so far as to propose an amendment that would have explicitly constitutionalized this interpretation by requiring the federal government to recognize and protect slavery in the territories.

As the mainstream political representatives of the antislavery movement, Republicans obviously had a quite different perspective on the problem. Their opposition to slavery was based on what I have described elsewhere as a theory of limited absolute equality—the idea that all men were equally entitled to a limited set of natural rights. Blacks could lay claim to fundamental rights not because racial discrimination was inherently wrong; rather, as one prominent Republican put it, with respect to the rights to life, liberty, and property, "it is a question of manhood, not of color."[43]

The themes that were later to be codified in the Fourteenth Amendment appeared often in Republican rhetoric. They argued that the provisions of the Fugitive Slave Act denied blacks due process of law; more radical elements led by Salmon P. Chase asserted that recognition of slavery in the territories was also inconsistent with the principles of substantive due process. In addition, antislavery forces contended that slaves were being denied the protection of the laws against their masters;[44] that antislavery agitators were denied the protection of law against mob violence;[45] and that even some free states denied blacks equal protection by refusing to acknowledge their right to contract and to hold property. Finally, some more advanced Republicans asserted that because free blacks were recognized as citizens in a number of northern states, state prohibitions on black immigration violated the comity clause, as did the oppressive negro seaman's acts adopted by some southern states.

In short, rather than being an open-ended assertion of broadly defined concepts, the language of section one taken in context emerges as a reference to well-established legal principles embodying the theory of limited absolute equality. Despite this historical background, a significant number of more extreme Republicans clearly took an expansive view of the import of the Fourteenth Amendment. Relying on the position of these Republicans, scholars such as Jacobus tenBroek,[46] Robert J. Kaczorowski,[47] and Harold M. Hyman and William M. Wiecek[48] have concluded that the Fourteenth Amendment (particularly when considered together with the Thirteenth Amendment) was originally understood to be a statement of general principles rather than a reference to specific rights. For a variety of reasons, however, the position of the Radical Republicans does not in itself offer solid support for those hoping to rely on the original understanding of the Fourteenth Amendment as the foundation for wide-ranging judicial interventionism.

First, during the early Reconstruction era, Radical Republicans were consistently outmaneuvered by more conservative forces in Congress, who sought to limit the scope of both statutory and constitutional change. The

Civil Rights Act of 1866 was passed only after the elimination of language that might have been construed to provide protection for rights beyond those specifically enumerated in the statute.[49] Similarly, Cong. John Bingham's initial draft of section one failed to win approval primarily because a number of influential Republicans feared that it would vest the federal government with authority over a wide variety of subjects that hitherto had been under the exclusive control of the states.[50] Finally, during the debates over the Fifteenth Amendment, conservative Republicans not only succeeded in preventing the adoption of more sweeping proposals, but also firmly rejected efforts to use the Fourteenth Amendment as a basis for a statute regulating suffrage.[51]

The political context in which the Fourteenth Amendment was drafted and adopted makes the dominance of conservative Republicans particularly significant.[52] Unlike the Thirteenth and Fifteenth amendments and the various civil rights bills passed during the post–Civil War era, the Fourteenth Amendment as a whole was not principally a response to a perceived need to protect and define the rights of individuals. Section one (together with section five) did empower the federal government to safeguard some of these rights. However, the provisions of section one were simply a part of an integrated Reconstruction plan that embodied the official position of the Republican party. The amendment was in essence a proposal for a peace treaty; if the South accepted it, congressional Republicans were willing to allow the governments of the defeated states to regain their status as full partners in the Union.

The Fourteenth Amendment was also designed to be a political statement to the voters of the North. In the congressional elections of 1866, Reconstruction was clearly to be the central issue. The amendment was drafted with an eye to its appeal to the northern electorate—especially those centrist "swing" voters whose support would be crucial to Republican success in the elections. Thus, for example, a proposal that would have required states to enfranchise blacks no later than 1876 was rejected because of the fear that it would cost the Republican party votes in a number of key northern states.

A second reason the arguments of the Radical Republicans are a weak basis for judicial interventionism is that they were typically aimed at defending a broad definition of the power of *Congress* rather than that of the federal courts. Indeed, contemporaries on all sides of the debate regarded section one as primarily a device for expanding congressional authority. Bingham himself described his motivation for proposing the Fourteenth Amendment in these terms:

The care of the property, the liberty, and the life of the citizen, under the solemn sanction of an oath imposed by your Federal Constitution, is in the States, and not in the Federal Government. I have sought to effect no change in that respect in the Constitution of the country. I have advocated [instead] an amendment which would arm Congress with the power to compel obedience to the oath, and punish all violations by State officers of the bill of rights, but leaving those officers to discharge the duties enjoined upon them as citizens of the United States by that oath and by that Constitution.[53]

Similarly, in rejecting a narrow reading of the amendment in 1879, the Supreme Court declared in *Ex parte Virginia* that the Reconstruction amendments "were intended to be, what they really are, limitations of the power of the States and enlargements of the power of Congress."[54] Viewed from this perspective, the Fourteenth Amendment was not a means to expand judicial authority but was actually a defense *against* the threat of judicial interventionism—the possibility (later realized) that civil rights legislation would be found unconstitutional on grounds that it was beyond the power of Congress.

Finally, even if one accepts the claim that the framers took an open-ended view of the judicial role under the Fourteenth Amendment, the original understanding would not *require* the adoption of an interventionist approach; instead, it would simply *permit* the federal courts to choose such an approach. The open-ended view holds that the framers did not intend to constitutionalize any particular analysis of the equal protection or privilege and immunities clauses. Indeed, the gravamen of the interventionist historical argument is that (in the words of Ronald Dworkin) the framers did not understand the language of the Fourteenth Amendment in terms of a rigorously defined conception of fundamental rights and equality but rather as referring to largely undefined concepts, leaving the judiciary to fill in the specific details. Presumably, in filling in these blanks, the framers would have expected the courts to choose the approach that would be best for society. Interventionists often argue that judicial enforcement of some relatively broad concept would lead to a more just society; yet if judges were to determine that a limited judicial role in defining equality and fundamental rights would yield better results for society, adoption of such an approach would also be consistent with an open-ended view of the original understanding.

The merits of the functional arguments in favor of judicial interventionism will be examined in the next chapter. For now, it is sufficient to note that *no* reading of the history of the Fourteenth Amendment *requires* widespread interventionism in order to implement the original understanding. Thus, unlike originalist interventionism, neo-originalist interventionism cannot be seen as a simple vindication of the legitimate authority of the framers to adopt binding legal rules.

APPROACHES BASED ON THE GENERAL POLITICAL THEORY OF THE FRAMERS

Other interventionists take a different path in seeking to tie their theories to the original understanding. Rather than focusing on specific constitutional provisions in isolation, these scholars contend that the Constitution *as a whole* can be viewed as the embodiment of a particular political theory. They claim that judicial interventionism is justified as a device to ensure that government operates in a manner consistent with that theory.

This argument is developed in the work of Cass R. Sunstein. Sunstein believes that the framers of the Constitution attempted to form a government that would follow the tenets of "classical republicanism"—a theory he describes as resting primarily on the requirement that government policies evolve through the process of "deliberation."[55] While conceding that the framers saw the political branches as the appropriate forum for this deliberation, Sunstein also contends that institutional and technological changes have undermined the ability of Congress and the president to perform the deliberative function. He concludes that "in these circumstances, it is neither surprising nor inappropriate that the judicial role has expanded and that some of the deliberative tasks no longer performed by national representatives have been transferred to the courts."[56]

Sunstein relies on this thesis to justify much of the constitutional program advocated by liberal interventionists. First, he suggests that the generally applicable rational-basis test be made more stringent.[57] Second, he asserts that the Court should apply a higher level of scrutiny "to cases involving the poor and other contexts—involving, for example, the mentally retarded and homosexuals—in which it seems likely that legislative outcomes will reflect existing relations of power."[58]

David A. J. Richards makes an analogous argument. Like Sunstein, Richards seeks to erect a constitutional structure based on the general political theory of the framers. Richards, however, claims that the overriding theme of the Constitution is "toleration"[59]—a principle derived from "the Lockean theory of political legitimacy, of the reasonable justification of state coercion of free and equal persons on terms of equal respect for rights in pursuit of the common interests of all."[60] Despite the different point of departure, Richards's policy prescriptions greatly resemble Sunstein's.

References to the political beliefs of the framers are not unique to neo-originalist analysis; indeed, they figure largely in originalism itself. Even the most committed originalist would accept the proposition that judges should sometimes refer to political understandings that were widely shared at the time of the drafting of the Constitution. The original understanding of a constitutional provision will at times not be immediately apparent from its language. In such instances, the understood meaning can only be divined by placing the provision in historical context. Often, contemporary political theories will be a critical part of that context. The pure originalist treatment of the Fourteenth Amendment is a classic example; as already noted, a limiting construction of the Fourteenth Amendment is possible only by placing section one in the context of Republican political thought.[61]

The neo-originalist approach of scholars such as Sunstein and Richards, by contrast, envisions a much broader use of the political principles of the framers. Rather than examining the theoretical background to provisions actually included in the Constitution, they argue that the justices should enforce the tenets of a given theory itself—even those tenets *not* specifically reduced to writing in the document. They apparently believe that this is a more appropriate definition of the "original understanding," but close examination reveals the flaw in their position.

The argument connecting the Sunstein/Richards approach to the originalist claim to legitimacy can be distilled to relatively simple terms. The framers did not adopt a constitutional text in a vacuum; instead, they chose particular provisions because they hoped and believed that the government created and limited by those provisions would function consistent with some political theory. Thus a true commitment to effecting the original understanding means striving to implement that theory as a whole, not simply the isolated understandings that support individual provisions.

Although this line of reasoning has some surface appeal, it rests on a fundamental misconception of the basic premises of originalism. The strength of originalist theory does not derive from the contention that courts should follow the general beliefs of those responsible for adopting the original Constitution and the amendments that have since been added to the document. Instead, the originalist claim is founded on the belief that judges should be bound by the rules that the framers incorporated in the charter of government through a legitimate lawmaking process. Conversely, unless a particular rule of law is adopted through the valid constitutionmaking procedures, it lacks the force of law. Thus, even if most or all constitutional provisions can be viewed as a product of a particular political theory, judicial enforcement of aspects of that theory not incorporated into the document is indefensible in originalist terms.

Here a statutory analogy is again instructive. Like constitutional originalists, judges interpreting statutes generally agree that they should be bound by the intent of the drafters.[62] By "intent," they do not mean the broad political theories that motivated the drafters in creating the statute; instead, they refer to the drafters' understanding of the rules that are embraced by the statutory language itself. The Civil Rights Act of 1964 is a prime example.[63] The drafters of the act were no doubt inspired by a general belief that persons should not be denied employment because of their membership in unpopular groups. By its terms, however, the act itself protects only *specific* groups from discrimination. Yet no one would claim that courts should seize on the underlying political conviction of the drafters as a reason to judicially extend the protection of the act to groups other than those listed in the statutory text.[64]

The same principles govern efforts to defend judicial interventionism based on the original understanding. The views of the framers of the Constitution are not to be followed for their own sake; instead, only the views included in the Constitution are to be granted the force of law. Thus, the appeal to some general political theory is appropriate only if it can be proved that the Constitution itself is an embodiment of that theory. The disarray among the commentators who rely on the framers' politics reflects the impossibility of identifying any single theory. Although Sunstein sees the framers as committed to classical republicanism, Ely argues that the Constitution was primarily aimed at establishing procedural fairness, and Richards sees the document as manifesting the concept of toleration. Admittedly, all these themes influenced the framers; for a variety of reasons, however, no one political or moral theory can adequately describe the Constitution in its full complexity.

THE PROBLEM OF THE MULTIPLE CONSTITUTION

One of the difficulties in identifying the political theory of the Constitution is that there is no single set of framers, or even a single time frame to serve as a point of reference. Although the original document was drafted in 1787, important parts of the modern Constitution were not included at that time—most notably, the Fourteenth Amendment, added after the Civil War. Since all the amendments were adopted at a later date than the original Constitution, the political theories embedded in them are likely to be different from those that animated the initial framers.

The position of the Constitution on the appropriate structure of government provides a useful example. The basic plan adopted by the 1787 convention left the states free to choose from among a wide variety of governmental structures, subject only to the vague admonition that they be "republican" in form.[65] Its description of the national legislature, by contrast, was far more detailed. The document specified a House of Representatives and a Senate. In the House of Representatives, the representation of each state was to be determined by the number of free inhabitants plus three-fifths of the number of slaves in the state. Control of the franchise was left to the states; those eligible to vote in state legislative elections were also to be eligible to vote for members of the House.[66] In the Senate, each state was to be represented by two senators elected by the state legislature. This plan reflected compromises on several issues, including the questions of whether representation should be apportioned by population or by state[67] and whether slaves should be included in the basis of representation.[68]

The terms of these compromises have been altered a number of times. After slavery was abolished by the Thirteenth Amendment, section two of the Fourteenth Amendment stipulated that blacks who were not allowed to vote would be excluded from the basis of representation. Section two was itself the product of delicate negotiations among adherents to a variety of different viewpoints.[69] Later amendments reduced state control over the election of federal (as well as state) legislators, prohibiting discrimination in the franchise on account of race[70] and sex,[71] outlawing the poll tax,[72] and requiring states to allow eighteen-year-olds to vote.[73] Another amendment provided for direct election of senators.[74] Congressional[75] and judicial decisions[76] have generated further modifications in the framework established in 1787.

The evolution of the Constitution's approach to these structural issues is archetypical of the process by which the document as a whole has developed. Because the components of the Constitution were adopted at different times, they were of necessity influenced by different political theories. Even if one focused on the provisions drafted within a narrow time frame, however, it would be impossible to identify a unified theory that adequately explains the shape of the Constitution. By their nature, constitutions are political documents, produced by political processes that inevitably involve compromises among different points of view. The forces that have generated these compromises in the American Constitution have varied, according to the particular constitutional provisions being considered.

THE POLITICAL COMPROMISES
OF THE 1787 CONSTITUTION

The drafters of the 1787 Constitution differed on virtually every important issue before the Constitutional Convention. Some believed in a strong central government, while others argued equally passionately for preservation of local autonomy; some believed that the federal legislature should be apportioned on the basis of population, and some that each state should have an equal voice in the legislature; some were proslavery and some antislavery. Moreover, taken alone, simple agreement among the delegates on the ideal form and limits of government was insufficient. The members of the convention also had to worry about the possibility that their handiwork would be rejected by a substantial number of states in the ratification process. The result of these conflicting pressures is a document that does not embody a single generalizable political theory; instead, the Constitution is best characterized as a series of specific compromises among a variety of different concepts of the nature and role of the federal government.[77]

The Federalist Papers clearly reflect a recognition of these compromises. *Federalist No. 37* discusses in detail the clash of interests facing the convention. Madison acknowledges first the "difficulties . . . in combining the requisite stability and energy in Government with the inviolable attention due to both liberty and the Republican form."[78] He then notes "the arduous . . . task of marking the proper line of partition between the authority of the general and that of the State governments,"[79] the "interfering pretensions of larger and smaller States,"[80] and the "other combinations, resulting from a difference of local position and policy [that] created additional difficulties"[81]—perhaps most notably, the split between North and South on slavery-related issues. Madison conceded that the interplay of these factors "forced [the Convention] into some deviations from that artificial structure and regular symmetry which an abstract view of the subject might lead an ingenious theorist to bestow on a Constitution."[82]

Each conflict paralleled a specific compromise embodied in the document that was finalized by the convention. *Federalist No. 39*, for example, examines the question of whether the new scheme of government should be considered "national" or "federal" and concludes that the plan produced by the convention "is neither a national nor a federal constitution, but a composition of both."[83] The discussion in *Federalist No. 62* describes the makeup of Congress as "the result of compromise between the opposite pretensions of the large and small States"[84] and notes pointedly that the principle of equal representation in the Senate was the political price for gaining the adherence of the smaller states to the new Constitution.[85]

Compromises were also evident on the slavery issue. First, the fugitive slave clause required free states to return escaped slaves to their masters.[86] In addition, although Madison called the slave trade a "barbarism of modern policy"[87] and conceded in *Federalist No. 42* that "it were doubtless to be wished that the power of prohibiting the importation of slaves had not been postponed,"[88] the federal government was denied this power until 1808 in order to mollify delegates from South Carolina and Georgia. Finally, the three-fifths compromise enhanced the political power of the slave states, even though Madison asserts in *Federalist No. 54* that the theoretical arguments in favor of counting slaves at all for purposes of determining representation are "strained."[89]

Despite these compromises, one central feature of the 1787 Constitution does emerge clearly. The document is not primarily a vehicle for the creation of rights *against* government. Instead, it is basically a power-granting instrument, expanding the scope of national authority and describing the processes by which that authority is to be exercised. This point is made strongly in *Federalist No. 41*, where Madison states that the Constitution should be considered, "FIRST, [as it] relates to the sum or quantity of power vested in the [federal] government, including the restraints imposed on the States [and] SECOND, [with respect to] the particular structure of the government and the distribution of this power among its several branches."[90]

The issue of individual rights per se is conspicuously absent from this characterization. This is not to say that the framers were not cognizant of the possibility that an overzealous federal government might be a threat to personal freedom; but, as Hamilton indicates in *Federalist No. 84*, most delegates initially believed that the basic concept of enumerated powers and the overall structure of the government would provide a sufficient safeguard against this danger.[91]

Of course, this aspect of the new Constitution was soon changed; the political clamor generated by the ratification process resulted in the addition of the ten amendments that form the Bill of Rights. As written, however, these amendments hardly give rise to the inference that they should be viewed as a mandate for open-ended judicial interventionism in support of some general political theory.

THE SIGNIFICANCE OF THE BILL OF RIGHTS

Any assessment of the significance of the Bill of Rights[92] to constitutional theory must address three separate aspects of the ten amendments. The first eight amendments deal with specific individual rights; the Ninth Amendment discusses the implications of the failure to address specific rights; and the Tenth Amendment confronts the relationship between the Constitution and state power generally. The relevance of the Ninth Amendment has already been discussed. The other two aspects have different implications for efforts to derive a general theory of rights underlying the Constitution.

The First Eight Amendments

Some commentators have attempted to rely on the first eight amendments as the source of a political theory that mandates nonoriginalist interventionism.[93] The argument of Ronald Dworkin is typical. Dworkin contends that when (anachronistically) linked with the equal protection clause, "the Bill of Rights . . . consists of broad and abstract principles of political morality, which together encompass, in exceptionally abstract form, all the dimensions of political morality that in our political culture can ground an individual right."[94] He further asserts that, taken together, these principles require "nothing less than that government treat everyone subject to its dominion with equal concern and respect."[95]

Justice Douglas's majority opinion in *Griswold v. Connecticut*[96] reveals a similar approach. In *Griswold*, the Court struck down a state statute that banned the use of contraceptives. Douglas conceded that nothing in the Bill of Rights explicitly mentioned a right to use contraceptives. Nonetheless, he found, when considered jointly, the First, Third, Fourth, Fifth, Ninth, and Fourteenth amendments created a "penumbra" that included a zone of privacy encompassing such a right.

Dworkin, Douglas, and others who seek to construct a general theory of rights from the first eight amendments must overcome a number of formidable obstacles. The first is the disparate nature of the rights protected by the Bill of Rights. The Fifth, Sixth, and Eighth amendments do seem to be related; when combined, they provide an outline for the appropriate conduct of criminal trials. Each of the other amendments, however, deals with a different problem. Some, such as the Third and Fourth amendments, were clearly responses to British governing practices that the former colonists had found distasteful. Others, such as the Seventh Amendment, protect rights that were deeply ingrained in English tradition. All protect specific interests rather than stating overarching principles of proper government.

The process by which the amendments were drafted also suggests that they responded severally to different issues. The Bill of Rights was sent to the states only after passing through ordinary legislative procedures, with numerous adjustments in language aimed at precisely defining the scope and import of each amendment.[97] Rejecting a proposal from Madison himself, Congress declined to adopt a sweeping declaration to the effect that "government is instituted and ought to be exercised for the benefit of the people; which consists in the enjoyment of life and liberty, with the right of acquiring and using property, and generally of pursuing and obtaining happiness and safety." Similarly, Congress also removed protection for a general right of conscience from what was to become the First Amendment.

In short, the structure and history of the Bill of Rights offer little comfort to those who seek to fit the Constitution into some easily defined political theory that would support neo-originalist interventionism. As Justice Douglas suggested in *Griswold*, some of the interests protected might seem to be at least loosely related; but although the import of some of the first eight amendments might be unclear at the margins, none implicitly or explicitly purports to bind the federal government to any general theory of rights.

The Tenth Amendment

The Tenth Amendment is frequently ignored in discussions of the Bill of Rights. It is, however, crucial to the evaluation of many noteworthy claims regarding a general theory of the Constitution. The amendment reserves to the state governments "the powers not delegated to the United States by the Constitution, nor prohibited by it to the States." This reservation embodies one of the most basic structural features of the Constitution—that the document is not designed to impose any general constraints on the states, only ones actually listed in the Constitution itself or adopted by Congress pursuant to its enumerated powers.

This point substantially undermines the claims of commentators who turn to some general political theory of the 1787 Constitution as support for nonoriginalist interventionism against state government action. The Tenth Amendment demonstrates that a key element of the thinking underlying the original Constitution was that states should remain free to act in the absence of *specific* federal prohibitions. Thus, even if a general theory of rights against the federal government could be found in the 1787 Constitution and the Bill of Rights, no similar theory would bind the state governments.

To summarize, the structure and background of the 1787 Constitution and the Bill of Rights are inconsistent with the claim that the document was perceived as giving legal sanction to some general theory of individual rights. But of course, the Constitution-making process did not end with the adoption of the Bill of Rights. Perhaps some later amendment incorporated just such a theory. The best candidates are the Reconstruction amendments adopted in the aftermath of the Civil War.

THE RECONSTRUCTION AMENDMENTS

By any standard, the Thirteenth and Fourteenth amendments[98] fundamentally restructured the American constitutional order. Each of these amendments guarantees individual rights; thus, on their face they seem to be a more promising well from which to draw rights-based theories of constitutional analysis. A closer examination, however, yields a different conclusion.

The Thirteenth Amendment

Some commentators have relied on the Thirteenth Amendment as evidence for an open-ended constitutional commitment to the concept of "freedom," broadly defined.[99] The amendment is an unlikely source from which to derive a basic constitutional theory. By its terms, the Thirteenth Amendment simply outlaws the institution of slavery; moreover, during consideration of the amendment, the Senate rejected substitute language proposed by Charles Sumner precisely because of its uncertain scope.[100] Admittedly, like many of the provisions of the Bill of Rights, the total import of the Thirteenth Amendment was unclear; at the same time, however, it can hardly be viewed as the pronouncement of some generalized political theory.

The Fourteenth Amendment

At first glance, section one of the Fourteenth Amendment might appear to be the most likely candidate for a constitutional provision from which to construct a broad theory of rights. Unlike the first eight amendments, it is apparently phrased in general terms (although, as I have argued previously, the drafters themselves probably viewed the language somewhat differently). Further, unlike the Ninth Amendment, the Fourteenth Amendment explicitly constitutionalizes the rights that it recognizes.

Initially, it should be noted that whatever theory one draws from the Fourteenth Amendment, it cannot plausibly be applied as a limit on the power of the federal government. As already noted, all parties to the debate over the amendment recognized that one of its primary purposes was to *expand* the scope of national authority.[101] Even as a restriction on state power, however, the Fourteenth Amendment was not the embodiment of a pure political theory but rather the product of compromises among a variety of positions.

Two conflicting ideological imperatives shaped section one. The Republicans who dominated the drafting process during the Thirty-ninth Congress were committed to the view that free blacks should be considered citizens and as such were entitled to federal protection of the fundamental rights of citizenship.[102] At the same time, however, most remained attached to the concept of states' rights and were deeply suspicious of measures that centralized authority in the federal government. The sentiments of the influential Sen. James W. Grimes of Iowa were typical on this point:

> During the prevalence of the [Civil War] we drew to ourselves here as the Federal Government authority which had been considered doubtful by all and denied by many of the statesmen of this country. That time, it seems to me, has ceased and ought to cease. Let us go back to the original condition of things, and allow the States to take care of themselves as they have been in the habit of taking care of themselves.[103]

The shape of the Fourteenth Amendment reflects the need to balance these ideological concerns, as well as the political pressures that beset the Republican party.

At the urging of Cong. John A. Bingham of Ohio, the Joint Committee on Reconstruction initially reported a measure that would have empowered Congress "to secure to the citizens of each State all privileges and immunities of citizens in the several States, and to all persons in the several States equal protection in the rights of life, liberty and property."[104] As noted earlier, Bingham explicitly disavowed any intention of divesting the state governments of primary authority to define and protect individual rights.[105] Despite these assurances, his proposal died on the floor of the House of

Representatives, primarily because of concerns that it would unduly expand the power of the federal government. Thomas T. Davis of New York summarized conservative Republican objections, complaining that "under [this proposal] the constitutional functions of State Legislatures are impaired, and Congress may arrogate those powers of legislation which are the peculiar muniments of State organizations, and which cannot be taken from the States without a radical and fatal change in their relations."[106] Similar sentiments were also expressed by such prominent Republicans as Sen. William M. Stewart of Nevada[107] and congressmen Roscoe Conkling[108] and Robert S. Hale of New York.[109]

After undergoing a number of changes in language during the deliberations of the joint committee, section one reemerged in its present form as part of an omnibus Reconstruction proposal. Defending the revised section, Bingham once again emphasized its consistency with traditional notions of federalism: "This amendment takes from no State any right that ever pertained to it. No State ever had the right, under the forms of law or otherwise, to deny to any freeman the equal protection of the laws or to abridge the privileges or immunities of any citizen of the Republic."[110] Their federalism-based concerns apparently satisfied by the new language, Republicans who had opposed Bingham's initial draft accepted the revised section one without comment.

The joint committee's treatment of the suffrage issue illustrated even more clearly the various tensions at work in the drafting process. At one point, the committee voted to include in the proposal a prohibition on racial discrimination in suffrage beginning in 1876. Political considerations, however, led the committee to replace this injunction with what is currently section two of the Fourteenth Amendment, which simply penalizes states that deny blacks the right to vote. The committee's report explained its actions:

Doubts were entertained whether Congress had power . . . to prescribe the qualifications of voters in a State, or could act directly on the subject. It was doubtful in the opinion of your committee, whether the States would consent to surrender a power they had always exercised and to which they were attached. As the best if not the only method of surmounting the difficulty, and as eminently just and proper in itself, your committee came to the conclusion that political power should be possessed in all the States exactly in proportion as the right of suffrage should be granted, without distinction of color or race. This it was thought would leave the whole question with the people of each State, holding out to all the advantage of increased political power as an inducement to allow all to participate in its exercise.[111]

This analysis attests to the complexity of the forces that gave rise to the final form of the Fourteenth Amendment. Rather than the embodiment of a pure theory of rights, it was also strongly influenced by elements of federalism and political expediency.

In short, the final form of the Fourteenth Amendment is best seen as a compromise between legislators with many different interests and viewpoints. Further, the process by which the Fourteenth Amendment was drafted stands as a paradigm for that of the Constitution as a whole; the document embodies a set of compromises generated by a set of legislative processes in many ways similar to those that generate statutes. Rather than *reflecting* a single, easily identified philosophical theory, the Constitution in effect *defines* a theory of government, influenced by a variety of sources but distinct from any of them individually.

The theory that interventionist judicial review should be designed to implement general political principles such as democracy, classical republicanism, or toleration does not reinforce the premises underlying the Constitution. Indeed, the theory undermines the one political premise that has been uniformly accepted by *all* supporters of the Constitution: that the framers of the Constitution had legitimate authority to make political decisions that would, at least in the absence of properly adopted constitutional amendments, bind government decisionmakers in the future. In requiring judges to act inconsistently with the compromises reached by the framers themselves, interpretive theories seeking the mandate of some broad political doctrine in essence reject the notion that the framers had such legitimate authority. Only pure originalism, which calls upon the courts to enforce those compromises, avoids this problem.

SIX

FUNCTIONAL DEFENSES
OF NONORIGINALIST INTERVENTIONISM

Unlike neo-originalism, the other major strand of nonoriginalist theory forthrightly rejects the originalist assertion that reliance on the original understanding is the sole legitimate justification for judicial interventionism. In most cases, adherents to this mode of nonoriginalist analysis concede that the original understanding is one valid source of authority for judicial interventionism. At the same time, however, they argue that other approaches have an equally strong claim to legitimacy and that originalism takes an unduly narrow view of the function of the judiciary in the American system. Beginning with this premise, nonoriginalists have devised a variety of different approaches that they contend would result in a better-functioning constitutional order.

On its simplest terms, this response to the legitimacy-based attack on nonoriginalist jurisprudence is entirely persuasive. Legitimacy is very much in the eye of the beholder; it is a premise rather than a matter capable of proof or disproof. Further, nonoriginalist arguments have played a significant role in constitutional discourse since judicial review became an accepted facet of the American system of government. Thus, if legitimacy is to be measured by historical pedigree, the original understanding is only one of numerous sources that can appropriately be consulted.[1] In short, the Borkian argument based on the concepts of neutrality and legitimacy cannot conclusively refute the claims of nonoriginalists.

Taken alone, however, this reasoning does not fully establish the case for nonoriginalist interventionism. Unlike originalists, who hold that the legitimate authority of the framers *requires* judicial interventionism, nonoriginalists generally claim only that legitimacy-related concerns are not a *bar* to the use of other approaches. Nonoriginalists must still make a positive case for the abandonment of originalist constraints on judicial decisionmaking.

Typically, nonoriginalist theorists take the position that an interventionist judiciary will enhance the performance of the governmental process and improve government decisionmaking. As will be seen, the putative benefits to be gained from judicial interventionism are questionable at best. But in any event, functional justifications must also take into account the costs stemming from an interventionist regime.

THE COSTS OF JUDICIAL INTERVENTIONISM

The most obvious costs generated by judicial interventionism are the transaction costs associated with the maintenance of any functioning judicial system. Put simply, interventionism by its nature encourages litigation, and litigation requires money to pay lawyers and judges and to support the complex judicial infrastructure. If the amount of litigation were reduced, the resources saved could be used to build roads, improve schools, or to address other pressing social problems.

In addition, interventionism increases undesirable uncertainty regarding the content of law. In order to adequately plan their lives, people need to know what legal rules will govern the consequences of their actions. Under a regime of constitutional interventionism, no legal rule is safe until it has run the full gauntlet of judicial review—a process that usually takes a number of years. By contrast, in a system governed generally by noninterventionist principles, actors can at least be certain that clear statutory rules will provide the measure against which their activities will be judged.

The most critical functional problem with interventionism, however, is its impact on governmental flexibility. Ironically, it is the defenders of nonoriginalist interventionism who often argue that a pure originalist approach unduly inhibits judicial adaptability. Nonoriginalists contend that originalist analysis leaves judges bound by the dead hand of the past. A more open-ended approach to judicial interventionism, they assert, leaves the judiciary free to make the appropriate adjustments necessary to "update" constitutional norms. As an indictment of originalist interventionism, this argument has considerable force; but as a justification for nonoriginalist interventionism, the flexibility-based argument lacks merit.

The basic flaw in the thesis is that it confuses the need for flexibility in government as a whole with the desire for judicial flexibility in constitutional adjudication. Without doubt, a large measure of decisionmaking adaptability is a preferred feature of any governmental system. Undue rigidity may inhibit the ability of government to adapt to changing conditions and to effect shared values. The required flexibility, however, need not be a function of shifting constitutional doctrine; instead, other branches of government might simply be left to change policy as relevant conditions dictate. From this perspective, open-ended interventionism does nothing to increase government flexibility.

Michael H. v. Gerald D.[2] provides an excellent illustration of this point. *Michael H.* was a California case arising from the efforts of a man to obtain legally enforceable visitation rights to the child of a woman who was married to a different man. In order to rebut the presumption of the husband's paternity, Michael sought to place into evidence a blood test that demonstrated that he was the biological father of the child. Under California law, however, only the mother or the husband was entitled to introduce such evidence. Michael argued that this restriction violated his Fourteenth Amendment rights.

By a five-to-four vote, the Supreme Court affirmed the California judgment. Speaking for a plurality, Justice Scalia made a classic noninterventionist argument.[3] He began by outlining a general methodology for determining if a particular right should be deemed fundamental, contending that the appropriate test was whether "the asserted liberty interest [is] rooted in history and tradition."[4] Applying this test to *Michael H.* itself, Scalia described the legal issue as "whether the relationship between persons in the situation of Michael and Victoria has been treated as a protected family unit under the historic practices of our society."[5]

To examine this question, Justice Scalia first canvassed the long history of the presumption of legitimacy, concluding that "even in modern times . . . the ability of a person in Michael's position to claim paternity has not been generally acknowledged."[6] In Scalia's view, moreover, even a demonstration that the right to establish paternity per se had been commonly recognized would be insufficient to establish Michael's claim; instead, in order to prevail, Michael would have to show that a person in his situation had traditionally been granted *parental rights*—that is, the right to participate in and in part control the upbringing of the child. Noting that "not a single case, old or new"[7] has granted such rights to someone in Michael's position, the plurality concluded that "this is not the stuff of which fundamental rights classifying as liberty interests are made."[8]

Obviously, Scalia's approach would allow little leeway for nonoriginalist interventionism. In dissent, Justice Brennan delivered a sharply worded interventionist attack on the plurality's analysis.[9] Relying heavily on the need for judicial flexibility, Brennan argued that Scalia's line of reasoning would render the substantive due process clause redundant with the political process, and he accused the justices in the plurality of conceiving of the Constitution as "a stagnant, archaic, hidebound document steeped in the prejudices and superstitions of a time long past" rather than a "living charter."[10] In defining fundamental rights, Brennan argued that the Court should focus on broad categories of liberty such as freedom from physical restraint, marriage, and childbearing. Continuing from this premise, Brennan implied that

Michael H.'s interest would be substantively protected under his approach. Appealing to the ideal of a "facilitative, pluralistic" society, he stated: "in a community such as ours, liberty must include the freedom not to conform"; Scalia's opinion, Brennan argued, "squashes this freedom."[11]

Brennan's analysis rests on two quite different concepts, both of which might be viewed as aspects of the need for flexibility. The invocation of the "living Constitution" rests on the need for *temporal flexibility*—that is, the idea that legal rules should be somewhat fluid so that they can be adapted to changing circumstances. By contrast, Brennan's emphasis on pluralism might be described as an appeal to *rule flexibility*—the notion that legal concepts should be structured to allow extensive freedom to choose among different moral value systems. Both temporal and rule flexibility are important elements of any well-designed legal system. Neither of these concepts, however, is advanced by a regime that countenances nonoriginalist interventionism. In fact, such interventionism actually interferes with both kinds of flexibility.

The main flaw in Brennan's analysis is that it fails to take into account the impact of judicial interventionism on other actors in the system. Admittedly, if the federal judiciary is considered in isolation, the portion of Brennan's argument based on temporal flexibility makes a lot of sense; Scalia's noninterventionist approach would clearly leave federal judges with little room to adjust constitutional standards in response to changing conditions. However, the increased judicial flexibility offered by the Brennan analysis would reduce the flexibility of other branches of government—in the case of *Michael H.*, the state governments. Scalia would leave the states free to determine parental rights based on the marriage-related claims of the mother's husband, the biologically based claims of the child's biological father, functional elements of the parent-child relationship, or any combination thereof. Brennan's analysis, by contrast, would have essentially forced the states to recognize (at least in some circumstances) the claims of a biological father in Michael H.'s position, even if they conflicted with the claims of the mother's husband. Thus, the states would have been deprived of significant options— the sine qua non of temporal flexibility.

In short, a methodology that allows nonoriginalist interventionism does not increase the temporal flexibility of the governing process but simply shifts the locus of flexibility from other branches of government to the federal judiciary. Moreover, the impact of this shift is not neutral, since interventionism has a negative effect on the overall temporal flexibility of the government decisionmaking process.

By their nature, constitutional judgments tend to be more static than other political decisions. The Supreme Court can certainly reverse itself and has shown an increasing willingness to do so in constitutional cases. However, the structure of government virtually guarantees that policy judgments premised on the authority of the Constitution will be more difficult to change than those finding their authority in other sources of law.

The mechanism of legal change in a noninterventionist world is relatively straightforward. If the legislature feels that a particular legal rule is outmoded or simply wrongheaded, it can simply adopt a statute that will alter the rule. For example, if the California state legislature could be convinced that biological relationships should invariably be the prime determinant of parental rights, the legislature could write that judgment into law, effectively reversing the *Michael H.* result.

The process of change becomes much more complicated where the legal rule at issue is established by an interventionist judicial decision. Suppose, for example, that Brennan's analysis had prevailed in *Michael H.* Presumably, the state legislature's first response would be to adopt a statutory scheme that would pass muster under his analytical framework. A later switch to a purely marriage-related model of parental rights would then require action by two separate governmental bodies. First, the state legislature would have to change its statutes again to reflect the marriage-related model—a change that, as will be discussed shortly, would be rendered substantially more difficult by the mere existence of a contrary interventionist decision. Second, the Court itself would have to reverse its prior position, holding the marriage-based statute constitutional. This two-step process is obviously more cumbersome than the simple method of legislative change, which establishes the conditions for temporal flexibility in a noninterventionist world. Thus, interventionism must be viewed as a barrier to such flexibility.

Nonoriginalist interventionism fares no better if one focuses on the need for rule flexibility. Here the problem is that Supreme Court decisions that invalidate state legislation effectively transfer decisionmaking authority from the state level to the federal level. This transfer inhibits the ability of state governments to adapt policy decisions to differing local value systems and to take into account local conditions in fostering shared values.

The Court's treatment of voluntary, race-based affirmative action programs is a prime example of this problem. American society is deeply divided on the desirability of these programs. In a noninterventionist world, state and local governments would have the freedom to shape their respective policies to conform to the attitudes of their constituencies, as well as to any special conditions that might counsel in favor of such programs. Yet the actual situation is quite different. In *University of California Regents v. Bakke*,[12] *Wygant v. Jackson Board of Education*,[13] and *City of Richmond v. J. A. Croson Co.*,[14] the Court invalidated affirmative action programs adopted by various units of state and local government. A majority of the justices in *Croson* held that strict scrutiny was the applicable standard, suggesting that most if not all such programs were unconstitutional. The result is that state and local governments have little latitude to take race into account in adapting to local conditions.

In short, rather than enhancing government flexibility, judicial interventionism actually diminishes that flexibility, adding substantially to the costs associated with such interventionism. In assessing the case for originalist interventionism, however, these costs are largely irrelevant. The justification for originalism does not hinge on the contention that the system will function more efficiently if government decisionmakers follow the original understanding. Instead, the argument is that the framers had legitimate authority to make rules governing the system and that because of that authority future decisionmakers are bound to follow those rules without regard to their efficacy.

Functional arguments in favor of judicial interventionism stand on a much different footing. Of course, the mere existence of costs does not prove that functional defenses of judicial interventionism must inevitably fail. It does, however, increase the burden of proof on those who would rely on them. Functionalists must demonstrate that judicial interventionism is likely to generate substantial advantages that outweigh the clear costs of that approach. The defenders of interventionism have made a number of different arguments in an effort to satisfy this burden.

These arguments must be evaluated at an appropriate level of generality. Obviously, all commentators believe that important societal benefits would ensue if the Court adopted their *specific* philosophical approach or political agenda. However, a defense of judicial interventionism cannot be premised on the belief that the justices will follow any particular mode of nonoriginalist analysis. It is unrealistic to assume that a conservative such as Antonin Scalia would embrace a jurisprudence based on the philosophy of toleration advocated by David A. J. Richards[15] or the feminist analysis of Sylvia A. Law.[16] Conversely, a liberal in the mold of William Brennan is equally unlikely to be in sympathy with Richard A. Epstein's strong aversion to economic regulation.[17] Thus the question must be phrased in broader terms:

whether overall, without assuming that the Court will adopt any specific approach, the results reached by a largely unconstrained interventionist judiciary are likely to provide significant benefits to society.

EXPANSION OF RIGHTS AS A BENEFIT

The crudest functional defenses of judicial interventionism rest on the perceived need to expand generally the scope of constitutional rights in the American system. For example, arguing in favor of nonoriginalist interventionism, Leonard Levy asserts that

> as government gets larger, more complex, more powerful, and more intrusive, the need to stay Caesar's hand increases. . . . Government power must be exercised in subordination to the right of the individual, as much as possible . . . The burden of proof should always be on government to show that rights claimed must be denied lest legitimate ends go unfulfilled because no alternative means are possible and the needs of the government compelling.[18]

Levy's argument rests on two assumptions. The first is that interventionism actually does expand the range of individual rights. The second is that the establishment of rights by the judiciary is generally a benefit to society. Both premises are seriously flawed.

First, even if one considers only so-called individual rights cases, interventionism will usually redistribute rights, not create a larger number of rights. The cases dealing with the rights of illegitimate children to inherit intestate from their natural parents provide a particularly clear example. Reversing an earlier decision that held states free to limit intestate succession rights to legitimate children,[19] in recent years the Court has consistently imposed severe restrictions on the ability of the government to differentiate between legitimate and illegitimate children in this regard.

Justice Brennan's opinion in *Labine v. Vincent*[20] explained the rationale for the later caselaw. He argued that "the formality of marriage primarily signifies a relationship between husband and wife, not between parent and child,"[21] which suggests that because the biological relationship with the father does not vary according to legitimacy, the rights of legitimate and illegitimate children should be presumptively equal. From this perspective, Brennan concluded that "the central reality of this case [is that the state] punishes illegitimate children for the misdeeds of their parents"[22] and that the statute "uphold[s] the untenable and discredited moral prejudice of bygone centuries which vindictively punished not only the illegitimate's parents, but also the hapless, and innocent, children."[23]

A detailed examination of the relationship between legitimacy and intestate succession reveals the error in Brennan's reasoning. Proper analysis of intestate succession begins with several fundamental observations. First, the amount of assets to be distributed is both finite and fixed. Second, in the absence of some state-enforced regime derived from either statute or common law, no person could establish a reliable, secure claim to any part of the assets. The purpose of any system of legal rules providing for the succession of property after the death of the owner is therefore to establish a priority among claimants. One generally recognized source of priority is a valid will executed by the decedent. Such a will can in whole or in part supersede other claims based on either the biological relationship between the decedent and the claimant or preexisting contractual arrangements between the decedent and the claimant. However, in intestate succession cases, the presumption is that no such will has been executed.

Under these circumstances, the claim of the illegitimate child of the decedent is based only on a biological relationship. Assuming that the legitimate child is also the biological offspring of the decedent, his or her biology-based claim is equal to that of the illegitimate child. But in addition, notwithstanding Brennan's view of which relationship is "primary" in a marriage, the legitimate child also has a contractually based claim derived from the marital contract between the parents. Nonetheless, the interventionist view is that the state must give no greater weight to the claim of a legitimate child than to that of a child born out of wedlock who can prove that he or she is the biological progeny of the decedent. This approach substantially dilutes the importance of the parent's marital contract to the claim of the legitimate child; indeed, under the interventionist view, the marriage has worth only as a device by which the legitimate child can prove a biological bond to the decedent.

Moreover, where claimants include both legitimate and illegitimate children, this approach will necessarily reduce the amount that the legitimate child would otherwise receive. For example, suppose the estate of the decedent is valued at $100,000. Suppose further that there are only two parties claiming the estate—one legitimate child and one illegitimate child. If only legitimate children are allowed to inherit intestate from their fathers, then the legitimate child will receive the full $100,000; if (as the interventionists would demand) the illegitimate child is treated as the equal of his or her legitimate counterpart, the legitimate child will receive only $50,000.

The situation can be further complicated if state law requires that the estate be divided between the decedent's spouse and children. The spouse's claim is derived entirely from the marital contract; as Justice Black noted in *Labine*, sexual relationships outside marriage typically do not give rise to intestate succession rights. The spouse's claim will be reduced by the amount awarded to legitimate children, whose claim can be traced not only to a biological relationship but also to the same contract or an analogous contract with a previous spouse. But if an additional amount is also granted to illegitimate children of the decedent, the share awarded under the marriage contract will be further reduced, once again lessening the importance of the marital relationship itself.

The lesson of the foregoing analysis is not to demonstrate that illegitimate children should not be allowed to inherit intestate. A governmental decision-maker might conceivably maintain that the biological tie between parent and child is so important that it should always be the predominant concern in intestate succession cases. The key point is that the interventionist approach to the intestate succession problem could not expand the total rights available; it could only redistribute a fixed set of rights.

As Robert A. Burt has demonstrated,[24] *Moore v. City of East Cleveland* provides a somewhat less obvious example. *Moore* was a challenge to a city ordinance that limited occupancy of a dwelling to members of a single family unit but defined "family" very narrowly. Under the ordinance, a grandmother was convicted for living with her son and two grandsons, who were first cousins rather than brothers. Three justices argued that the relationship between the grandmother and grandchildren was entitled to no special constitutional protection, and they voted to uphold the judgment of the lower court.[25] A majority of the Court rejected this view, however, and by a five-to-four margin the conviction was reversed.

Justice Powell's plurality opinion took an interventionist tack, contending that the ordinance should be subject to stringent judicial scrutiny. Powell rested this assertion on the idea that the rights protected under substantive due process analysis extend beyond the bounds of the traditional nuclear family to other biological relationships:

Ours is by no means a tradition limited to respect for the bonds uniting the members of the nuclear family. The tradition of aunts, cousins, and especially grandparents sharing a household along with parents and children has roots equally venerable and equally deserving of constitutional recognition. . . . Even if conditions of modern society have brought about a decline in extended family households, they have not erased the accumulated wisdom . . . that supports a larger conception of the family.[26]

After considering state interests in preventing overcrowding, minimizing traffic and parking congestion, and avoiding an undue burden on the local school system, Powell concluded that they were insufficient to justify the ordinance.[27]

The opinion of the interventionist plurality in *Moore* ignored the rights of the remaining residents of the city. Justice Powell argued that the issue in *Moore* was whether a city could "standardiz[e] its children—and its adults—by forcing all to live in certain narrowly defined family patterns."[28] This description of the issue, while in some respects accurate, tends to obscure the major effect of the holding that the ordinance was unconstitutional. Whatever the result in *Moore*, Mrs. Moore and her two grandsons could no doubt have maintained themselves as a living unit somewhere in the Cleveland metropolitan area; the only question in the case was whether they would be allowed to do so in East Cleveland. The real issue in *Moore* was not whether Mrs. Moore and her grandsons would be forced to conform to a standardized mold; rather, it was whether a small segment of society— the residents of East Cleveland—could decide that they wished to reside in an area characterized by the presence of nuclear families and could protect that preference by defining their community so as to exclude people whose style of living did not fit that pattern.[29] Powell's discussion of congestion and the burden on the school system touches on this question only tangentially, if at all, thus leaving the rights of anyone other than Mrs. Moore virtually unconsidered.

In short, the contention that judicial interventionism will generally expand the universe of rights available in society is at best questionable. But even if it were credible, Levy's position is substantially overstated. For not even the most aggressive interventionist would claim that *all* rights-favoring decisions by the Court have benefited society. Among the most prominent examples have been cases establishing constitutional rights to hold slaves in federally administered territories;[30] to work for less than a minimum wage;[31] to freely choose whether or not to have an abortion;[32] to attend desegregated schools;[33] and to be treated no less favorably by the government than members of minority racial groups that have historically faced discrimination.[34]

Few if any would consider all these interventionist decisions correct. Thus any functional defense of interventionist theory based on the need to expand rights must ultimately rest on the view that federal judges are uniquely suited to decide *which* rights should be expanded.

One approach—adopted by a number of noted justices—has been to argue that the Court is well placed to protect those values that are "deeply rooted in this Nation's history and tradition" and/or comport with widely shared "contemporary norms."[35] Even leaving questions of competence aside, such appeals to tradition and consensus cannot adequately justify nonoriginalist interventionism. The mere fact that a value has traditionally been or is currently associated with American culture does not necessarily mean that respect for that value will improve the overall quality of governmental decisionmaking. Thus, in order to justify nonoriginalist interventionism, one must also demonstrate that the judgments made by the Court are likely to be in some sense "better" than those made by other branches of government.

Many interventionist theories rely on precisely this argument. For example, Owen Fiss states that unlike legislatures, which "see their primary function in terms of registering the actual, occurrent preferences of the people," courts are "ideologically committed [and] institutionally suited to search for the meaning of constitutional values."[36] Likewise, Ronald Dworkin claims that

> judicial review insures that the most fundamental issues of political morality will finally be set out and debated as issues of principle and not simply as issues of political power, a transformation that cannot succeed, in any case not fully, within the legislature itself. . . .   [It] called some issues from the battleground of power politics to the forum of principle. It holds out the promise that the deepest, most fundamental conflicts between individual and society will once, someplace, finally, become questions of justice.[37]

Fiss, Dworkin, and similarly inclined commentators[38] subscribe to a view that might be described as constitutional moralism. The essence of their position is that because the justices of the Supreme Court are insulated from ordinary political pressures, they are uniquely well-positioned to bring moral insights to bear on questions of basic values. In one sense the moralists are clearly correct; judges are less subject to partisan pressures than most other governmental decisionmakers in American society. This does not necessarily imply, however, that they will reach more reliable decisions on basic moral issues than other officials. Indeed, one would expect that a decisionmaker freed from outside constraints would simply implement his or her own personal value judgments. The crucial question is whether there is any reason to believe that judges would behave differently.

One possibility is that judges might be specially trained to evaluate competing moral claims through extensive study of philosophy, theology, anthropology, sociology or psychology. But appointment to the federal bench requires expertise in none of these fields (or, for that matter, in any other discipline relating to policymaking generally). Instead, the usual qualifications are: that the person be well-connected politically; that the person share the same basic political philosophy as the president; and, if the appointment is to be considered a "good" one, that the person have demonstrated mastery of the art of manipulating the technical rules of the law. None of these characteristics suggests that judges will have any special expertise in divining moral "truth."

The last characteristic does, however, indicate the ways in which judicial analysis of policy questions differs substantially from that of other branches of government. As already noted in chapter 2, society as a whole emphasizes the importance of distinctively legal conventions in judicial proceedings; the law school education that all judges have received reinforces the influence of such conventions on the decisionmaking process. The result is that Supreme Court justices often reach conclusions different from ones that they would have drawn if free to act as legislators. These conclusions will generally not, however, be driven by special moral insights; instead, they will reflect the judge's willingness to *ignore* his or her view of the relative merits of competing moral claims in favor of legal convention.

Holmes's *Lochner* dissent[39] illustrates this well. While his ultimate conclusion is entirely consistent with most mainstream constitutional scholarship, his methodology was antithetical to the argument that the justices are well-positioned to make fundamental moral judgments for society. The conventions invoked by Holmes rest on the *opposite* premise—that other branches of government should make these judgments and that judges should respect the judgments because of their own institutional role in the system. It is this perception of institutional limitation, rather than any special moral expertise, that sets judges apart from other government decisionmakers. Thus there is no theoretical support for the moralist view that judges will come to more accurate conclusions on basic moral issues.

The moralist position might still be sustained if it could be shown that on balance nonoriginalist interventionism has *in practice* been a force for moral advancement. Such an argument requires a two-step analysis: first, identifying the nature of "moral advancement"; and second, demonstrating that the Court's decisions have contributed to that progress. The first problem is clearly daunting, as different segments of society hold dramatically different perceptions about morality.[40] Some, for example, hailed the recognition of abortion rights in *Roe v. Wade* as a major advance, while others saw the same decision as an abomination. For purposes of testing the moralist hypothesis, however, one might well define "moral growth" as advancement of positions consistent with contemporary American liberalism. Despite the renascence of the conservative interventionist movement, most modern commentators who take the moralist position would probably still accept this characterization.

Accepting this standard for the sake of argument, there are two possible approaches to evaluating the impact of judicial interventionism on American society. Initially, the moral tone of American society could be compared to that of societies sharing much of the Anglo-American heritage but lacking a strong tradition of aggressive judicial interventionism. Alternatively, the content of interventionist decisions themselves could be examined to determine if the positions they espoused promote the moral development of society. Measured against either of these standards, the evidence in support of the moralist position is at best inconclusive.

To my knowledge, no prominent moralist has made the kind of detailed comparative study necessary to prove that American society is more morally advanced than its counterparts in the Western world. Admittedly, one can readily identify specific elements of some advanced societies that left/center theorists would find distasteful: the existence of an Official Secrets Act and lack of an exclusionary rule in Great Britain are obvious examples. At the same time, however, Mary Ann Glendon has argued that judicial review has actually retarded the development of moral analysis in American society on such issues as abortion and homosexuality.[41] In any event, it seems clear that at this stage, comparative inquiry has not supplied the necessary evidence to justify moralist claims.

A detailed evaluation of the Court's performance is equally unavailing for moralists. Focusing only on the Warren and early post-Warren eras, judicial interventionism did indeed favor left/center values.[42] A longer view, however, reveals this period to be something of a historical anomaly. In this regard, a full canvass of the Court's treatment of race-related issues is particularly useful.

Moralists argue that the unanimous decision in *Brown v. Board of Education of Topeka*,[43] which outlawed state-imposed racial segregation, cannot be justified by originalist legal convention, and they often point to the decision as the crowning achievement of their approach to constitutional adjudication. As I have explained in detail elsewhere, in my view *Brown* can be defended in originalist terms.[44] Even if the moralist analysis of *Brown* is correct, however, the case cannot be considered in isolation; taken collectively, the Court's handling of the race question has been much less consistent with left/center premises.

The best contemporary example is, of course, the decision in *City of Richmond v. J. A. Croson Co.*[45] There the Court struck down a program which required that those contracting with the city government subcontract no less than 30 percent of the total value of the contract to minority-owned subcontractors. At the margins, the precise implications of the *Croson* holding are somewhat uncertain; what is clear is that a majority of the justices are committed to the proposition that race-conscious affirmative action programs should be subjected to stringent judicial scrutiny. Although *Croson* will undoubtedly be viewed by some as a vindication of the general concept of race-blindness,[46] the principle on which the decision is based is repugnant to the left/center perspective.[47] The rejection of this perspective is by no means a historical aberration. The more distant past discloses clear examples of cases in which the Court either actively supported racism or thwarted the efforts of other government bodies to free blacks from oppression.

In the antebellum era, *Prigg v. Pennsylvania*[48] and *Dred Scott v. Sandford*[49] stand out. In *Prigg*, the Court struck down state laws designed to protect fugitive slaves living in free states from being seized by their erstwhile masters. *Dred Scott* went even further; rejecting the plaintiff's efforts to use the federal courts to secure his freedom, Chief Justice Taney's lead opinion concluded that descendants of slaves could never be citizens of the United States *and* that the federal government lacked constitutional authority to bar slavery from the territories it governed.

After the Civil War and the adoption of the Reconstruction amendments, judicial decisions became a significant obstacle to legislative efforts to ease some of the worst burdens of racism. Congress adopted a series of statutes intended to implement the Thirteenth, Fourteenth, and Fifteenth amendments; the Court, however, gave only a grudging reading to the newly granted federal authority. For example, in *United States v. Reese*[50] the Court severely restricted congressional authority to protect voting rights, and in the *Civil Rights Cases*,[51] it held that Congress had no power to reach private racial discrimination. Thus in this context it was the legislature that took the morally correct posture toward racism and the judiciary that created barriers.

These examples should not be construed to imply that the actions of the Court have invariably supported racism. The point is that, taken as a whole, the actions of the judiciary cannot be accurately characterized as either consistently proracist or antiracist. Instead, like that of government as a whole, the performance of the Court is best described as uneven—not a very surprising conclusion, since Supreme Court justices are not apolitical. Rather, they bring to the bench the same basic beliefs held by the segment of the governing elite of society from which they are drawn. If, as Fiss, Dworkin, and other moralists propose, they are freed from the constraints of legal convention (or even when the impact of such constraints is unclear), each justice can be expected to implement those shared beliefs—not the ideal morality advocated by one moral philosopher or another.[52]

The Supreme Court's decisions on modern issues such as school desegregation and race-based affirmative action provide a particularly instructive example of the dynamic of the judicial policymaking process in the absence of strong constraints. In these cases, the Court acted on politically charged issues without discernible guidance from originalist principles. Further, unlike the nineteenth-century decisions, the doctrine in both groups of cases clearly showed a change in judicial attitude during a relatively short period of time. Thus, a close study of these changes and the circumstances surrounding them offers a model case study of the performance of an unconstrained judiciary dealing with controversial moral questions.

In the early post-*Brown* period (approximately 1954–1964), disagreements over desegregation cut across party lines. The divisions instead were sectional, with northern public opinion typically endorsing the idea of desegregation (at least in principle) and the majority of white southerners opposing it. During this period, adherents to the northern ideology dominated the Court completely; although southerners Hugo Black and Thomas C. Clark were members of the Court, they had been appointed by Democratic presidents who shared the basic northern view. Thus, predictably, the Court's pronouncements in the school desegregation cases not only imposed progressively more stringent requirements on previously segregated schools but were almost without exception decided by unanimous votes.

Beginning in 1964, the political landscape of the desegregation issue changed dramatically. While not explicitly endorsing a return to legally imposed racial segregation, the forces dominating the national Republican party became committed to limiting the authority of the federal courts to prescribe sweeping remedies in school desegregation cases. National Democrats, by contrast, had an equally deep commitment to strong measures designed to achieve racial balance in schools. Until 1968, this political shift had little impact on the behavior of the Court; Democrat Lyndon B. Johnson was president, and his appointments to the Court generally agreed with the prodesegregation ideology of the sitting justices.

In 1969, however, the change in the political dynamic of school desegregation began to have an effect on the Court itself. From 1968 to 1975, the presidency was held by Richard M. Nixon and then, from 1980 to 1988, by Ronald Reagan, Republicans who shared a strong ideological commitment to restricting the scope of desegregation relief. Together they appointed seven justices whom they hoped would reshape the approach of the Court on this issue. By 1992, it was clear that this effort had met with a large degree of success.

The transformation was admittedly gradual. In 1969 and 1970, Nixon appointed Warren E. Burger and Harry Blackmun to replace Earl Warren and Abe Fortas, respectively. One year later, the Court unanimously held in *Swann v. Charlotte-Mecklenburg Board of Education*[53] that lower courts were justified in imposing a sweeping reorganization on a school district in order to remedy the effects of earlier state-imposed segregation. Even the appointments of Lewis F. Powell and William H. Rehnquist did not immediately reverse the tide; in 1973, *Keyes v. School District No. 1*[54] established evidentiary rules that opened the way for extension of *Swann*-type orders to northern, urban school districts that had never formally adopted a rigid system of racial segregation in education.

Even in *Swann* and *Keyes*, however, the impact of the change in the mix of political views on the Court was becoming apparent. Burger, the author of the majority opinion in *Swann*, was instrumental in forcing the inclusion of a declaration that the Constitution does not require racial balance per se in schools.[55] This principle was to assume great significance in later desegregation litigation. Further, in *Keyes*, Burger, Powell, and Rehnquist declined to join the majority opinion, with Powell and Rehnquist filing opinions explicitly questioning the reasoning of the majority.[56] These opinions marked the first major crack in the hitherto-solid pro-integration stand of the justices.

The Nixon appointees' first notable victory in the school desegregation dispute came in *Milliken v. Bradley*.[57] Building on *Swann*'s rejection of racial balance as a constitutional standard, the Court in *Milliken* held by a five-to-four vote that in most cases school desegregation remedies could not mandate consolidation of school districts or transportation of students across school district lines. The split on the *Milliken* Court reflected the importance of the political background of the judges in determining their approach to cases where distinctively legal principles do not yield clear answers: the dissenters were all Warren Court holdovers, while the majority was composed of the four Nixon justices plus Potter Stewart, an Eisenhower appointee who had been one of the most conservative justices on the Warren Court.

Despite the *Milliken* result, the political viewpoint of the dissenters in the case continued to be a crucial influence on the school desegregation decisions of the Court for many years thereafter. Three of the four dissenters in *Milliken*—William J. Brennan, Thurgood Marshall, and Byron R. White—remained on the Court at least through 1990. They found a reliable ally in John Paul Stevens, appointed to replace William O. Douglas in 1975 by Gerald Ford—a Republican president who was much less of an ideologue on school desegregation than either Nixon or Reagan. The perspective of this group became a majority in 1979 when Nixon-appointee Blackmun crossed over to their side in *Dayton Board of Education v. Brinkman*[58] and *Columbus Board of Education v. Pennick*,[59] which extended the *Keyes* principles and guaranteed that virtually every major urban center in the North would be faced with *Swann*-type desegregation decrees. The power of this new coalition was felt as late as 1990, when in *Spallone v. United States*[60] the same five-member majority reaffirmed in sweeping terms the broad authority of the district courts over school policies in areas under desegregation orders.

By contrast, on the issue of dissolving desegregation injunctions, the views of the Nixon appointees (and the successors selected by Reagan) gained and held the upper hand. In 1976, White joined the members of the *Milliken* majority to limit the remedial powers of the federal courts in *Pasadena City Board of Education v. Spangler*.[61] The Court concluded that a school board that had initially complied with a court desegregation order specifying the proportion of minority students in each of its schools cannot be required to alter attendance zones each year in response to local population changes. Counterbalancing Blackmun's defection, in 1990 White joined Rehnquist and Reagan appointees Sandra Day O'Connor, Antonin Scalia, and Anthony Kennedy in *Board of Education of Oklahoma City Schools v. Dowell*,[62] where the majority articulated relatively lenient standards for measuring the degree of compliance that would justify the dissolution of the initial injunction. The trend continued in *Freeman v. Pitts*,[63] in which an even more conservative Court once again approved the partial dissolution of a *Swann*-type order.

In the school desegregation context, the shift from a Court dominated by liberal justices to one in which more conservative jurists were ascendant led to a decrease in judicial interventionism. On the question of the constitutionality of classifications designed to provide advantages to minority races, it had quite the opposite effect. As conservative influence increased, the Court became more actively involved in striking down initiatives adopted by other branches of government.

The Court did not address the constitutionality of voluntary affirmative action programs until 1978—well after the Nixon appointees had changed the complexion of the bench. The first two important decisions—*University of California Regents v. Bakke*[64] and *Fullilove v. Klutznick*[65]—were decided by a Court composed of three Democrats who at that time had records suggesting sympathy for the interests of minorities (Brennan, White, and Marshall); four Republicans who had been appointed by Nixon (Burger, Blackmun, Powell, and Rehnquist); one Republican appointed by Eisenhower (Stewart) and one by Ford (Stevens). As in the school desegregation context, the voting pattern of the justices reflected, not great moral insight, but rather the political background of the individual justices.

In some respects, the breakdown of the votes in these cases is the mirror image of the pattern in the school desegregation cases. Each of the Democrats voted to reject both constitutional challenges; by contrast, with the exception of Justice Blackmun, all of the Republicans looked on the programs with some degree of suspicion. Even so, the dynamic that generated the pattern of results on the affirmative action issue is more complicated than that in the desegregation cases.

One of the major reasons for this complexity is timing. Affirmative action did not emerge as a burning issue on the political scene until the early 1970s. Thus, before Nixon, presidents could hardly have been expected to take the justices' views on the question into account when making their appointments. Further, even during the Nixon presidency, the division between the political parties on affirmative action had not become clear-cut; for example, Nixon's own administration was quite active in promoting race-conscious plans that benefited minority groups.[66] For this reason also, the justices were chosen without specific emphasis on their positions regarding the constitutionality of affirmative action programs. It should therefore not be surprising that all of the Republican justices except Rehnquist and Stewart exhibited considerable ambivalence when addressing *Bakke* and *Fullilove*.

While the *Bakke-Fullilove* Court did not find all race-conscious affirmative action constitutionally unobjectionable, the results of the two cases were largely acceptable to the constituencies that supported such programs. However, the election of Ronald Reagan in 1980 placed all these plans in potential constitutional jeopardy. Unlike Nixon and Ford, Reagan was firmly opposed to racial preferences and could be expected to appoint justices who shared that resolve. Yet in the first six years of his two terms, Reagan could do little to move the Court in this regard. The only retirement was that of Potter Stewart, and his replacement—Sandra Day O'Connor—was actually marginally less hostile to affirmative action programs than Stewart had been. In 1986 came the decision in *Wygant v. Jackson Board of Education*,[67] the first case in which a majority of the Court found a race-conscious plan unconstitutional. The outcome in that case, however, was dictated not by the change in the Court's membership but rather by the defection of Powell and White from the *Bakke* and *Fullilove* majorities.

With the replacement of Burger and Powell by Scalia and Kennedy, the influence of Reagan's approach to affirmative action became stronger. In *City of Richmond v. J. A. Croson Co.*, both new appointees expressed their belief that race-conscious affirmative action programs were generally unconstitutional,[68] and it became clear that when such a scheme was adopted by states or their subdivisions, it would almost certainly be struck down by the Court. Because White has a different perspective on programs established by the *federal* government, in 1990 five votes were still available to validate some (but not all) federal affirmative action programs—as the decision in *Metro Broadcasting Corp. v. FCC* demonstrated.[69] However, the subsequent replacement of Brennan and Marshall by David H. Souter and Clarence Thomas, respectively, places even this limited use of race-based affirmative action programs in constitutional peril. Indeed, the change in personnel has already had an impact; in *Shaw v. Reno*[70] the Court limited the use of race-conscious remedies under the Voting Rights Act. In any event, it seems apparent that the Court has moved sharply to the right on the affirmative action question since the initial *Bakke* and *Fullilove* holdings.

Although any number of lessons might be drawn from the development of the constitutional law of race relations, one point emerges clearly: there is no reason to believe that the relaxation of institutional constraints on the judiciary would improve the overall moral tone of government decisionmaking. Instead, as political scientists have observed,[71] an unconstrained Court would likely become a device by which presidents could impose their views on future policymakers through carefully chosen appointments who would remain on the Court long after the presidents themselves had left office. Of course, other factors might enter the picture as well. A particular justice might disappoint the president's expectations; new issues not contemplated by the president might come to the Court; or the president might simply choose not to focus on specific ideological commitment in making his choice. But these factors do not augur for an increase in the moral sensitivity of the Supreme Court's decisionmaking process; they simply inject an element of randomness into that process.

Given this reality, there is a certain dissonance in the pattern of the scholarship dealing with the special competence of judges to make moral decisions. Despite the recent emergence of commentators such as Epstein, Siegan, and Barnett, advocacy of unconstrained judicial interventionism remains primarily the province of leftist voices in the academy. Conversely, the primary defenders of noninterventionism are prominent conservatives, such as Bork and former attorney general Edwin Meese. Yet if the current chief justice and his ideological allies were to accept completely the interventionist arguments regarding the superior faculty of the judiciary to make basic moral judgments, the resultant interventionism would almost certainly concentrate on even greater protection for property rights and limitations on economic regulation—constitutional principles that would be anathema to most left/center and leftist theorists. Conservatives who have consistently supported judicial restraint might derive some perverse pleasure from this outcome, but it would not be in the best interest of the political system as a whole, given the costs associated with judicial interventionism.

JUDICIAL INTERVENTIONISM AND THE QUALITY OF POLITICAL DIALOGUE

A second common functional defense of judicial interventionism is based on a weaker claim regarding the competence of the Court to deal with fundamental values.[72] Theorists who rely on this premise do not claim that the judiciary will generally make better decisions on basic moral questions. Instead, they argue that nonoriginalist interventionism improves the decisionmaking process by adding a different, distinctive voice to the dialogue that ultimately creates governmental policy. This position stems from one view of the interaction between the courts and other branches of government, which was perhaps best articulated by the late Alexander Bickel:

Virtually all important decisions of the Supreme Court are the beginnings of conversations between the Court and the people and their representatives. They are never, at the start, conversations between equals. The Court has an edge, because it initiates things with some immediate action, even if limited. But conversations they are, and to say that the Supreme Court lays down the law of the land is to state the ultimate result, following upon a complex series of events, in some cases, and in others it is a form of speech only.[73]

Taken alone, Bickel's conception simply describes the impact of judicial review on the overall decisionmaking of government. Others, however, have elaborated on the idea in an attempt to justify judicial interventionism. The argument of Michael J. Perry is typical:

In the constitutional dialogue between the Court and the other agencies of government—a subtle, dialectical interplay between Court and polity—what emerges is a far more self-critical political morality than would otherwise appear, and therefore likely a more mature political morality as well—a morality that is moving (inching?) toward, even though it has not always and everywhere arrived at, right answers, rather than a stagnant or even retrogressive morality.[74]

Similar themes can be found in the works of a number of other commentators.[75]

The evolution of constitutional death penalty jurisprudence provides an excellent example of the process envisioned by those who embrace the Bickel/Perry model of judicial review. In 1972, a majority of the Supreme Court invoked the Eighth Amendment to strike down all then-existing capital punishment statutes in *Furman v. Georgia*.[76] While two members of the five-justice *Furman* majority would have found capital punishment unconstitutional per se,[77] the other three limited their opinions to the specific statutes before them.[78]

In response to *Furman*, many states reinstituted capital punishment but modified the rules for determining when the imposition of the death penalty was appropriate. Beginning in 1976, the Court considered the revised schemes, finding some constitutional and some not.[79] As states gradually conformed their legislative and judicial procedures to the decisions of the Court, the death penalty reemerged as a fact of American life; the formal prerequisites for imposition of the penalty were, however, quite different from those that had governed the pre-*Furman* era.

Rather plainly, the Supreme Court did engage in a conversation with the state legislatures on the death penalty issue. Such a conversation takes place even when—as in the case of school prayer[80]—the Court does not change its ultimate conclusion. As Herbert Wechsler has pointed out, "to say that [the Court] initiates a dialogue is not, of course, to say that it is necessarily attentive to its critics."[81] The point is that constitutional decisions are not set in stone; if criticisms from the populace and other branches of government are sufficiently cogent, the Court may be persuaded to alter its position.

The mere fact that a dialectical relationship exists does not, however, justify nonoriginalist interventionism. Given the costs associated with judicial intervention, dialogue theorists must also demonstrate that such interventionism improves the overall quality of the debate. Neither sound theory nor practical experience supports this claim.

Dialogue theories implicitly proceed from an inaccurate perception of the position courts would occupy in a nonconstitutional world. The assumption seems to be that in the absence of judicial review, the courts would have little input into the governmental debate over major ethical questions. This supposition ignores the impact of judicial decisions in common law and statutory contexts.[82] Although legal conventions clearly affect the development of caselaw in these situations, such decisions are also often strongly influenced by the same ethical arguments to which legislatures might respond in the lawmaking process.

The interpretation of Title VII of the Civil Rights Act of 1964[83] illustrates this point in a statutory setting. Two of the key issues have involved the effect of the statute on discrimination against pregnant workers and the role of discriminatory impact in the statutory analysis. On both issues, the development of legal principles reflected a true dialogue between Congress and the Supreme Court.

The Supreme Court first addressed the pregnancy issue in *General Electric Co. v. Gilbert*.[84] Employees challenged a disability plan that provided benefits for nonoccupational sickness and accidents but excluded pregnancy from its coverage. Speaking for the majority, Justice Rehnquist argued that the plan did not discriminate "on the basis of sex"; instead, he characterized the discrimination as being between pregnant persons and nonpregnant persons—both male and female.[85] Thus the majority concluded that the exclusion did not violate Title VII.

Congress responded to *Gilbert* by passing the Pregnancy Discrimination Act of 1978 [the Pregnancy Act],[86] which provides that

> the terms "because of sex" or "on the basis of sex" include . . . because of or on the basis of pregnancy, childbirth, or related medical conditions; and women affected by pregnancy . . . shall be treated the same for all employment-related purposes, including receipt of benefits under fringe benefit programs, as other persons not so affected but similar in their ability or inability to work.

The full import of the statutory change was made clear in *Newport News Shipbuilding and Drydock Co. v. EEOC.*[87] After the passage of the Pregnancy Act, the employer in *Newport News* had amended its health benefits plan to furnish coverage for pregnancy-related expenses of female employees but not those of the spouses of male employees. Tracking the majority argument in *Gilbert*, the employer argued that male employees were discriminated against, not because of their sex, but rather because they themselves could not become pregnant. Under this interpretation, the Pregnancy Act would have been viewed as intending only to overrule the specific holding in *Gilbert* and guarantee that female employees would be entitled to medical benefits for pregnancy. Rejecting this contention, the *Newport News* majority opined that Congress meant to overturn generally the conclusion that pregnancy-based discrimination was not sex discrimination.[89] Thus, the exclusion of coverage for spousal pregnancies was found to be illegal sex discrimination.

The development of the law of disparate impact reflects a somewhat different dynamic. The original legislative history of Title VII on this point contains substantial evidence that Congress aimed to prohibit only intentional discrimination.[88] Nonetheless, in *Griggs v. Duke Power Co.*,[90] the Court held that because an employment test disqualified blacks in disproportionate numbers, the test could not be used absent a showing of "business necessity." When amending Title VII in 1972, Congress apparently acquiesced in this interpretation.[91] Almost twenty years later, in *Wards Cove Packing Co. v. Atonio*,[92] the Court held that the *Griggs* test was less stringent than many had assumed. This holding sparked a renewed debate in the political branches over the appropriate standard to be applied in disparate impact cases, culminating in the passage of the Civil Rights Restoration Act of 1991, which explicitly restored disparate impact analysis to the position that it had occupied before *Wards Cove*. However, the Court was given no clear guidance on the nature of the burden of proof faced by the employer.

The treatments of the pregnancy and disparate impact issues illustrate two models in the nonconstitutional dialogue between the courts and the legislature. In both cases, Congress initiated the dialogue when it passed Title VII. The Supreme Court then addressed a moral issue inherent in the language of Title VII—in one case, the meaning of discrimination on the basis of sex, and in another, the disparate impact question. On the pregnancy issue, Congress responded by adopting a different definition of sex discrimination, and the Court deferred to the congressional definition. On the disparate impact issue, Congress accepted the Court's approach; then, after the Court had modified it, Congress reinstated the original approach by statute. But in each case the ultimate legal resolution of the moral issue emerged after a conversation between the legislative and judicial branches.[93]

The key difference between this dialogue and that created by constitutional decisionmaking is that in the statutory context it is clearly the legislature rather than the judiciary which has the last word. Of course, even in the statutory process, the judiciary has a tremendous influence on the ultimate conclusion, as the *Griggs* example demonstrates. Once the courts have interpreted a statute, that interpretation can only be overturned by a concerted legislative effort. Moreover, the mere fact that the judiciary has declared its understanding may make such an effort more difficult to mount; its interpretation will carry a certain moral force that may tend to deter attempts at legislative change.

When the Court relies on constitutional arguments to intervene, the impact of its decision on the debate will be magnified. One can, of course, accurately observe that constitutional judgments are not always the final word on moral issues. At the same time, however, it is clear that, unlike statutory or common law decisions, such judgments cannot be overturned by the ordinary legislative process. Moreover, a court's decision to speak in the name of the Constitution adds tremendously to the weight of its conclusions on the debate. Thus the effect of constitutionally based judicial interventionism is not simply to allow courts to participate in the deliberation of moral questions but rather to give judges an enormous advantage over other participants in the debate.

The establishment of such a judicial advantage can only be justified if two conditions are satisfied. First, the judges must bring a *unique* perspective to the debate over fundamental issues of public policy. Second, there must be some reason to believe that that perspective is somehow superior to the viewpoint of other governmental decisionmakers and thus leads to an improvement in the overall decisionmaking process. On the presumption of uniqueness, dialogue theorists face the same difficulties confronted by constitutional moralists: nothing in the training or institutional position of judges would suggest that their decisions or reasoning bring any new vision to the fore. This conclusion is reinforced by the actual results of the Court's attempts to deal with controversial, important moral issues.

Three of the most significant recent examples involve abortion, capital punishment, and the use of racial classifications favoring historically disadvantaged groups. In each case, the Court has dealt with the controversy in many different contexts, with a pattern of results that has changed over time as the political balance of the Court has changed. The opinions issued by the various justices have reflected many different perspectives. Some of the justices have grappled skillfully with the moral questions involved; others have been almost painfully clumsy. In none of these examples, however, has judicial interventionism made a unique contribution to the societal dialogue.

The discussions of abortion and capital punishment by the noninterventionist justices do share one characteristic that is peculiar to the judicial process—a heavy emphasis on institutional concerns. Rather than directly analyzing the specific moral questions that are before the Court, these opinions typically rely primarily on the theory that the Court is not the appropriate body to make final judgments on such controversial moral/political topics. Obviously, arguments against judicial interventionism generally do not enhance society's understanding of specific issues such as abortion and capital punishment. Thus, this feature of judicial decisionmaking cannot by itself vindicate the claims of dialogue theorists.

By contrast, the interventionist justices—those who would strike down the abortion and capital punishment statutes before the Court—focus heavily on discussions of the moral questions presented by such statutes, as do the justices on both sides of the controversy over race-based affirmative action. These opinions do not, however, add significantly to the general comprehension of the issues; instead, the analysis in these opinions differs little from that which takes place in other branches of government or in society at large. Consequently, they also fail to advance the political dialogue in any meaningful sense.

Indeed, because of its impact on the legislative process, judicial interventionism actually damages the quality of debate over fundamental moral questions. As a result of the near-mythic stature of the Supreme Court in

American society, the simple assertion that a position is unconstitutional—i.e., inconsistent with the announced doctrine of the Court—is considered a sufficient rebuttal to any argument for legislative action to promote that position. The result is that opponents of the policy are largely relieved of the responsibility for developing the moral justification necessary to defend their stance.

The repercussions of the Court's decision to intervene in the abortion controversy illustrates this point. Between 1973 and 1988, if a prolife legislator had introduced a bill to ban all abortions, it is unlikely that prochoice opponents would have entered into an extended discussion of the moral questions at issue. Instead, they would simply have cited *Roe v. Wade* and contended (correctly) that the proposal was unconstitutional. The debate would thus be reduced to a matter of citation of legal authority.

The *Roe* decision also damaged the political dialogue over abortion in other respects. In the five years before *Roe* (and the Supreme Court's entry into the picture), the state legislatures had gradually been moving toward the relaxation of the requirements for a legal abortion. Five states had adopted the position that abortions could be performed for any reason; two others allowed abortions to preserve the life or health of the mother.[94] The most popular reform, however, tracked the Model Penal Code, which provided that abortions would be lawful in any one of a number of circumstances: if the continuance of the pregnancy posed a substantial risk of gravely impairing the physical or mental health of the mother or of ultimately producing a child with a grave physical or mental defect; or if the pregnancy resulted from rape, incest, or other felonious intercourse.[95] This pattern of reform (and in some cases lack of reform) reflected the classic American legislative process, which often arrives at compromise even on issues that involve deeply felt moral values.

Roe had the effect of polarizing the debate. Fortified by the oracular authority of the Court, prochoice forces could now claim not only that their position was objectively correct but also that support for legal limits on abortion was inconsistent with the most basic values underlying American society. Conversely, prolife elements were outraged that *Roe* had placed the imprimatur of the Constitution on a practice that they believed was fundamentally immoral. The result was that both sides began to resist adamantly even the most minor, reasonable concessions to the opposing viewpoint.

While the decisions of the Court in *Roe* and its progeny put constitutional law into the service of prochoice values, the prolife groups were initially quite successful in winning political tests of strength with their prochoice counterparts.[96] The signal success of the anti-abortion forces came with the passage of the Hyde Amendment. Before 1973, federal funds had been available to pay for abortions whenever such abortions were legal under state law.[97] Under the Hyde Amendment, use of federal funds was barred except in limited circumstances involving rape and incest and in those cases in which the life of the mother was threatened.[98] These restrictions were held to be constitutional in *Harris v. McRae*.[99]

Although it did alter the politics of the issue, the Court's decision to retreat from *Roe* in *Webster v. Reproductive Health Services* and *Planned Parenthood of Southeastern Pennsylvania v. Casey*[100] did nothing to repair the damage to the dialogue that had been caused by *Roe*. Indeed, if anything, the new decision to defer in some measure to the judgment of other branches of government inflamed passions even further. Prolife groups understood that, in order to achieve victory, they also had to succeed in the political process. Conversely, threatened with the loss of judicial protection against governmental action regulating what a seemingly authoritative source had held to be their constitutional birthright, prochoice groups redoubled their efforts to ensure that legislators would adopt the most extreme version of their viewpoint. Compromise (and even intelligent discussion) seems as far away as ever.

Even if *Roe* were completely overruled in a post-*McRae* world, the prochoice movement is almost certainly in a better legal position than it was before 1973. The key point, however, is not one of substance but of process. As the abortion cases reveal, the ability of judicial activism to raise the level of debate over moral issues is wildly uncertain. Thus, even from a purely empirical perspective, any justification for judicial interventionism grounded on the view that interventionism improves the overall quality of political dialogue is problematic at best.

JUDICIAL REVIEW AND THE STRUCTURE OF GOVERNMENT

The other major functional justification for judicial review is the cornerstone of John Hart Ely's representation-reinforcement theory. Ely contends that the courts should use the power of judicial review to make certain that each resident has equal influence in the overall decisionmaking process of government. Beginning with this premise, he argues that the federal courts should actively intervene in two classes of cases. First, they should ensure that the representatives of the various units of government are selected in a manner consistent with the principle of one person, one vote. Second, the courts should give special constitutional protection to "discrete and insular minorities"—aliens, women, and members of minority races, for example— whose influence is unfairly diminished by the operation of even democratically elected legislatures.[101]

Ely's defense of his theory actually combines both neo-originalist and functional elements. He first argues that the Constitution was primarily designed to establish procedural fairness, including "broad participation in the processes and distribution of government."[102] In addition, he contends that regulation of the political process is a task the judiciary is particularly well-positioned to perform; Ely believes that, unlike other functionally justified theories of nonoriginalist interventionism, his approach does not require judges to make substantive value judgments.[103] The last of these claims is the easiest to dismiss. As any number of Ely's critics have pointed out, the preference for representative democracy is clearly a subjective, substantive value judgment.[104] A successful defense of representation-reinforcement analysis must depend on the remaining two justifications.

The neo-originalist aspect of Ely's argument is also unsound. His claim that the Constitution reflects democratic theory is based on a fundamental misconception regarding the structure of the document. The Constitution does indeed deal extensively with questions of suffrage and representation. Yet taken together, the provisions handling these issues paint a picture quite different from that described by Ely.

Admittedly, the framers of the 1787 Constitution made frequent references to the idea that government derived its legitimate authority from the primal power of the people. As already noted, however, the framers defined "the people" much more narrowly than do late twentieth-century advocates of democracy. For example, while conceding that "it is certain, in theory, that the moral foundation of government is, the consent of the people," John Adams also argued that it was not necessary that "old and young, male and female, as well as rich and poor must consent, expressly, to every act of legislation." Women were to be denied the suffrage because "nature has made them fittest for domestic cares" and left them unfit for "the great businesses of life, and the hardy enterprises of wars, as well as the arduous cares of state." Children, servants, and the propertyless were also not to be entrusted with the ballot; they were "too little acquainted with public affairs to form a right judgment, and too dependent upon other men to have a will of their own."[105] Although suffrage qualifications varied from state to state, this philosophy was reflected in whole or in part by all state governments. Thus, only about one American in six was eligible to vote during the founding period.[106]

Moreover, representatives of the politically powerful classes that drafted the Constitution had good reason to fear the unrestrained forces of democracy. States where popularly elected governments reigned supreme had seen strong challenges to the rights of property that the framers believed should be inviolate. The desire to strengthen the federal government was partly a reaction to these attacks.[107] Finally, as with all constitutional provisions, issues of states' rights weighed heavily in the framers' calculations. The state governments were hardly likely to support a federal constitution that intruded significantly on their ability to frame their own governing institutions as they saw fit. In addition, many representatives of the smaller states insisted on a decisive voice for the states in the structure of the federal government itself.

All these influences were reflected in the final form of the Constitution. While the House of Representatives was to be chosen by "the people," access to suffrage was not universal but limited to those possessing "the qualifications requisite for electors of the most numerous branch of the State Legislature." The states were also explicitly left entirely free to set up the process by which the members of the electoral college were to be chosen. Finally, the Senate was expressly designed to be a check on the excesses of democracy.[108]

The situation is only slightly less clear with respect to the state governments. The Constitution does guarantee to states a "republican" form of government, but given the wide variety of state governments in place during the late eighteenth century—all of which were apparently considered republican in form—this qualification cannot have been viewed as inconsistent with even the most vaguely representative structure. The reference to state voting procedures in the provisions for election to the House of Representatives implicitly confirms this observation.

Ely, however, does not rely solely on the 1787 Constitution in making his argument; instead, he seeks to link the guarantee of a republican form of government with the equal protection clause in an effort to develop a constitutional principle supporting "a political process open to all on an equal basis."[109] However, this argument also meets with substantial historical difficulties. As has already been demonstrated in chapter 5, the framers of section one of the Fourteenth Amendment explicitly disclaimed any intention to encroach on state control over suffrage. Admittedly, in section two of the amendment, the framers did attempt to encourage expansion of the suffrage by adjusting the basis of representation in the House of Representatives. Even there, however, the commitment to representative democracy was tempered by the first explicit constitutional recognition that women and aliens could be denied the vote without penalty—a fact that was decried by the feminist movement of the time and its allies among the radical wing of the Republican party.[110]

Although much less widely discussed than the genesis of the Fourteenth Amendment,[111] the evolution of the Fifteenth Amendment provides an even clearer picture of the interaction among political theories and practical realities that shaped the stance of Reconstruction Republicans on the suffrage issue. The Fifteenth Amendment is particularly instructive for two reasons. First, the debates over the amendment and possible alternative formulations were unusually extensive. Second, during those debates a serious drive was mounted to constitutionalize the precept that legislative selection should be based on purely democratic principles. This was the only time in American history that such an effort was seriously considered by Congress.

Republicans generally agreed on one important ideological principle: that federal action was necessary to prohibit explicit exclusions of free blacks from the right to vote. Further, although the rights of blacks were clearly the central concern of Republicans, they refused to limit the proposed constitutional amendment to blacks, rejecting outright proposals to exclude the Chinese from its coverage. Thus, it can be fairly said that the Republican commitment extended beyond protection of blacks to the prohibition of racial discrimination generally. Republicans split sharply, however, over proposals to expand the voting rights amendment to cover other types of discrimination.

The key proposal designed to effect the principle of one person, one vote, was made by Sen. Henry Wilson of Massachusetts. Wilson would have barred denial of the right to vote or hold office on the basis of race, color, nativity, property, education, or creed.[112] Sen. John Sherman of Ohio aptly summarized the theory underlying Wilson's plan:

It seems to me, as the Republican party are about to lay the foundation for a political creed, that the broadest and best foundation for it is universal suffrage, protecting all men above the proper age and with the proper residence in the right to share in the elective franchise and the right to hold office. . . . I am willing myself to accept as a party creed the broad general principle that every man of a given age and prescribed residence shall have an equal voice in making the laws and enforcing the laws of the United States.[113]

At one point Wilson's proposal actually passed the Senate.[114] However, during the complicated parliamentary maneuvering that followed, it fell victim to a number of different objections. Some legislators favored restricting the suffrage on principle. For example, attacking the Wilson scheme, Sen. James W. Patterson of New Hampshire expressed his support for literacy tests:

> The voter discharging the obligation of an elector fulfills an official duty as truly as the judge exercises the functions of an office when he administers justice between man and man; and as some knowledge is a prerequisite in the judge to the proper discharge of his duties, so it would seem that some intelligence, some mental discipline, some little knowledge of the laws and spirit of a country is necessary to a safe participation in its government.[115]

Others voiced federalism-related objections to the Wilson language; thus, Sen. Roscoe Conkling of New York complained that it would "revolutionize and undo the constitutions, the enactments, and the customs of the States."[116] Still another group of legislators based their judgments on political expediency; while affirming his personal preference for the constitutionalization of universal suffrage, Cong. Benjamin F. Butler of Massachusetts supported a narrower amendment because it had the best chance of passage.[117] All these influences ultimately combined to lead Congress to reject universal suffrage proposals.

The constitutional picture that emerges from the combination of the 1787 Constitution and the Reconstruction amendments is thus very different from Ely's portrayal. Rather than describing a regime based broadly on the principle of one person, one vote, the Constitution creates a system in which primary control over the structure of government is vested in the states, subject only to specific, limited exceptions imposed by the document itself. The five subsequent amendments cited by Ely also fit comfortably into this pattern, since they do not place sweeping constraints on the structure of state government but simply specify additional, narrowly tailored exceptions to the general principle of state control.[118] Thus, representation-reinforcement analysis cannot claim to be merely an elaboration of the original understanding.

Ely's functional justification for interventionism to protect the rights of discrete and insular minorities also falters under the burden of proof. The difficulties with his analysis are especially evident in his treatment of discrimination against aliens. Ely contends that because aliens cannot vote, they present a "relatively easy case" for special judicial solicitude to ensure that their interests are properly considered.[119] However, denying aliens the right to vote reflects a judgment that people who owe allegiance to some other government are not entitled to have their interests weighed in the deliberations of the government of the United States. One can, of course, dispute this reasoning;[120] but in that case the remedy is to require that aliens be enfranchised, not to make the Court assume the role of surrogate guarantor of their just treatment.

Ely, however, is concerned not only with cases in which groups are barred from participation in the political process. He also argues for judicial interventionism to secure the rights of groups such as women and homosexuals, whose influence he believes has been diluted by prejudice.[121] Even accepting his view that this kind of legislative market failure is of constitutional magnitude, the Court is not well-placed to redress this imbalance. While the decisions of the political branches of government may not reflect equal consideration of the interests of all citizens, decisions of the justices are hardly likely to be more accurate.

First, because the justices are drawn from the governing elite, they are unlikely to be free from the prejudices that infect the judgments made by their peers in other branches of government. For example, until the last few decades, women and homosexuals were in fact largely voiceless in the political arena, and the Court was of no help to them. It was only after the feminist and gay rights movements had achieved a measure of political prominence and legislative success that the justices began to take their claims seriously. Put another way, an unconstrained Court is much more likely to aid the newly powerful rather than the truly powerless.

Further, the nature of the litigation process itself will frequently make the Court institutionally unfit to properly assess the full range of concerns raised by the claims of Ely's discrete and insular minorities. Often, the only parties before the Court will be the government and the member of the disadvantaged minority. Given this posture, the Court will almost inevitably view the case before it in terms of the relationship between the rights of the minority and some vaguely defined governmental interest. The contingent interests of other parties who might be affected by the judgment will be ignored or downplayed.

Consider, for example, *Frontiero v. Richardson*,[122] one of the seminal cases establishing the principle that laws discriminating on the basis of gender would be subject to heightened scrutiny. In *Frontiero*, the Court struck down a statute that granted all servicemen the right to claim their wives as dependents for purposes of receiving increased benefits but allowed a servicewoman to claim her spouse as a dependent only if she supplied more than one-half of his support. The plurality seemed to assume that as a result of the decision, the government would require *all* members of the armed services to prove that their spouses were actually dependent in order to obtain the increased benefits.[123] In fact, given the political realities, it was far more likely that all married members of the armed services would be allowed to receive the benefits. In that case, the main beneficiaries of the *Frontiero* decision would be servicewomen whose husbands were not in fact dependent on them, and the decision would obligate the government to pay the claims of these women.

The necessary resources to pay these new claims might be raised through a variety of means. The benefits of other members of the service might be reduced; funds might be taken from other governmental programs; or taxes might be raised. The difficulty is that the *Frontiero* Court itself had no control over or even knowledge of the source of funds to be tapped to cover the added expense. Lacking such information, the Court was hardly in a position to evaluate either the moral force of the servicewoman's claim or (in Ely's system) the conclusion that might be reached by a perfectly functioning democratic system of government.

The other branch of the representation-reinforcement argument—that judges should police the structure of government itself—stands on somewhat better footing. The functional defense of this aspect of Ely's theory rests on the observation that judges have a much smaller personal stake in the composition of government than other potential decisionmakers. Of course, judges bring idiosyncratic political theories and personal predilections to the decisionmaking process, but unlike legislators, federal judges do not depend on the election process to maintain their positions. Therefore, on paper at least, they are better placed to decide issues of apportionment and voting rights. Thus, unlike other theories of nonoriginalist review, this narrow version of representation-reinforcement analysis can claim a plausible functional justification.

The difficulty is that this role for the federal courts also collides directly with the legitimate authority of the framers of the Constitution itself. With respect to congressional elections, the Constitution quite clearly vests the state governments with authority over the "time, place and manner of holding elections,"[124] subject only to *congressional* supervision and the proviso the voter qualifications shall be the same as those for the most numerous branch of the state legislature. Similarly, since the framers of the Fourteenth and Fifteenth amendments specifically considered and rejected proposals to impose sweeping restrictions on state legislatures, the Tenth Amendment must be viewed as barring federal judicial action to prescribe constraints beyond those specified in the Constitution itself. Thus, in this case, judicial action would manifestly be not only "extraconstitutional" but "contraconstitutional" as well.[125] Given this state of affairs, the legitimacy-based arguments that support originalist interventionism weigh equally heavily against Ely's approach.

CONCLUSION

Constitutional theory has reached a critical stage in its development. Proceeding from widely shared but fundamentally misconceived premises, originalist and nonoriginalist analysts have been equally unsuccessful in creating intellectually satisfying models describing the appropriate role of judicial review in the American governmental system. If true progress is to be made in constructing such a model, theorists must abandon conventional wisdom and reorient their thinking in new directions.

First, concerns regarding "legitimacy" should no longer be the central focus of discussions of nonoriginalist interventionism. While admittedly significant, questions of legitimacy have absorbed nonoriginalists to the point that they have failed to put forth a plausible reason for the courts to adopt an interventionist approach in any but the most narrowly defined class of cases. Given the costs inevitably associated with judicial interventionism, appeals for such intervention must founder in the absence of compelling justification.

Originalists face a different problem. Although the appeal to the legitimate authority of the framers does provide the necessary rationale for judicial interventionism, the argument proves too much: the same argument that justifies interventionism in individual rights cases would also require the Court to limit sharply the power of the federal government to regulate the economy. Thus, the major difficulty with originalism is that, in practical terms, it would allow the judiciary to intrude unduly into the functioning of government in the modern world.

Finally, and perhaps most important, all constitutional theorists must disabuse themselves of the notion that an unconstrained judiciary would inevitably favor some particular political position or persuasion. Both the theory and practice of judicial review suggest that the impact over time of an interventionist judiciary is completely unpredictable. Only when this fact is fully recognized and integrated into constitutional analysis can an adequate theoretical structure be built.

NOTES

PREFACE

1. 476 U.S. 276 (1986).
2. 488 U.S. 469 (1989).
3. See, for example, Michel Rosenfeld, "Decoding Richmond: Affirmative Action and the Elusive Meaning of Constitutional Equality," *Michigan Law Review* 87 (1989): 1729–94; Kathleen M. Sullivan, "Sins of Discrimination: Last Term's Affirmative Action Cases," *Harvard Law Review* 100 (1986): 78–99.
4. David Chang, "Discriminatory Impact, Affirmative Action, and Innocent Victims: Judicial Conservatism or Conservative Justices," *Columbia Law Review* 91 (1991): 790–844.
5. Ibid., p. 792 n. 6.
6. Ibid., p. 842 (emphasis in original).
7. The results of this research are described in detail in Earl M. Maltz, *Civil Rights, the Constitution, and Congress, 1863–1869* (Lawrence, Kans., 1990).

CHAPTER 1. THE POLITICAL DYNAMIC OF CONSTITUTIONAL THEORY

1. 112 S. Ct. 2791 (1992).
2. 476 U.S. 747 (1986).
3. 462 U.S. 416 (1983).
4. *Philadelphia Inquirer*, 30 June 1992, p. A10.
5. 198 U.S. 45 (1905).
6. Christopher G. Tiedman, *A Treatise on the Limitations of Police Power in the United States* (1886; repr. New York, 1971), vii-viii.
7. Charles G. Haines, *The American Doctrine of Judicial Supremacy* (1932; repr. New York, 1973), p. 450.
8. Quoted in ibid., p. 15.
9. Laurence H. Tribe, *American Constitutional Law*, 2d ed. (Mineola, N.Y., 1988), p. 581 and sources cited therein.
10. E.g., Carter v. Carter Coal Co., 298 U.S. 238 (1936); Railroad Retirement Board v. Alton Railroad Co., 295 U.S. 330 (1935).
11. E.g., NLRB v. Jones & Laughlin Steel Co., 301 U.S. 1 (1937); West Coast Hotel v. Parrish, 300 U.S. 379 (1937).
12. Tribe, *American Constitutional Law*, pp. 582–83.
13. See, for example, R. Kent Greenawalt, "The Enduring Significance of Neutral Principles," *Columbia Law Review* 78 (1978): 982–1021; Herbert Wechsler, "Toward Neutral Principles of Constitutional Law," *Harvard Law Review* 73 (1959): 1–35. The limitations inherent in the concept of neutrality are explored in Cass R. Sunstein, "Neutrality in Constitutional Law (with Special Reference to Pornography, Abortion, and Surrogacy)," *Columbia Law Review* 92 (1992): 1–52.
14. See Liva Baker, *The Justice from Beacon Hill: The Life and Times of Oliver*

Wendell Holmes (New York, 1991); Paul L. Murphy, *The Constitution in Crisis Times, 1918–1969* (New York, 1972), p. 15.

15. E.g., Alexander M. Bickel, *The Least Dangerous Branch: The Supreme Court at the Bar of Politics* (Indianapolis, 1962); Wechsler, "Toward Neutral Principles of Constitutional Law."

16. 347 U.S. 483 (1954).

17. E.g., Reynolds v. Sims, 377 U.S. 533 (1964) (Warren, C.J.) (state legislature must be apportioned according to principle of one person, one vote).

18. See, e.g., Plyler v. Doe, 457 U.S. 202 (1982) (Brennan, J.) (Constitution limits power of states to discriminate against undocumented aliens); San Antonio Independent School District v. Rodriguez, 411 U.S. 1 (1973) (Brennan, J., dissenting) (voting to invalidate school financing system based on property taxes).

19. See Zorach v. Clauson, 343 U.S. 306 (1952) (states may constitutionally accommodate religion).

20. See Doe v. Bolton, 410 U.S. 179, 209–21 (1973) (listing wide range of rights that Douglas believes should be accorded special constitutional protection).

21. See Adamson v. California, 332 U.S. 46, 68–123 (1947) (Black, J., dissenting).

22. See, e.g., Roth v. United States, 352 U.S. 964 (1957).

23. See, e.g., Mapp v. Ohio, 367 U.S. 643 (1961) (application of Fourth Amendment exclusionary rule to states).

24. E.g., Duncan v. Louisiana, 391 U.S. 145 (1968); Miranda v. Arizona, 384 U.S. 436 (1966).

25. E.g., Harper v. Virginia Board of Elections, 383 U.S. 663 (1966); Reynolds v. Sims, 377 U.S. 533 (1964).

26. Griswold v. Connecticut, 381 U.S. 479 (1965).

27. See *New York Times*, 22 May 1969, p. 46, and 23 May 1969, pp. 26 and 27.

28. This phenomenon has become increasingly apparent in recent years. See the statistics collected at *Harvard Law Review* 102 (1988): 351; *Harvard Law Review* 101 (1987): 363; and *Harvard Law Review* 100 (1986): 305.

29. Earl M. Maltz, "Portrait of a Man in the Middle—Mr. Justice Powell, Equal Protection, and the Pure Classification Problem," *Ohio State Law Journal* 42 (1979): 941–64.

30. E.g., San Antonio Independent School District v. Rodriguez, 411 U.S. 1 (1973).

31. E.g., Dandridge v. Williams, 397 U.S. 471 (1970).

32. E.g., Roe v. Wade, 410 U.S. 113 (1973).

33. E.g., Craig v. Boren, 429 U.S. 190 (1976).

34. E.g., Trimble v. Gordon, 430 U.S. 762 (1977).

35. E.g., Graham v. Richardson, 403 U.S. 365 (1971).

36. 410 U.S. 113 (1973).

37. 1980 Republican Platform, in *Congressional Quarterly Almanac* (Washington, D.C., 1980), vol. 36, p. 62–B; 1984 Republican Platform in *Congressional Quarterly Almanac* (Washington, D.C., 1984), vol. 40, p. 55–B.

38. 1980 Democratic Platform, in *Congressional Quarterly Almanac* (Washington, D.C., 1980), vol. 36, p. 106–B; 1984 Democratic Platform, in *Congressional Quarterly Almanac* (Washington, D.C., 1984), vol. 40, p. 93–B.

39. E.g., Ann E. Freedman, "Sex Equality, Sex Differences, and the Supreme Court," *Yale Law Journal* 92 (1984): 913–69; Sylvia A. Law, "Rethinking Sex and the Constitution," *University of Pennsylvania Law Review* 132 (1982): 955–1040.

40. See, e.g., Webster v. Reproductive Health Services, 109 S. Ct. 3040 (1989)

(abortion); Stanford v. Kentucky, 109 S. Ct. 2969 (1989) (death penalty); Kadrmas v. Dickinson Public Schools, 487 U.S. 450 (1988) (free transportation to public schools).

41. David A. J. Richards, *Toleration and the Constitution* (New York, 1986).

42. Judith A. Baer, *Equality under the Constitution: Reclaiming the Fourteenth Amendment* (Ithaca, N.Y., 1983), p. 105.

43. Michael J. Perry, *The Constitution, the Courts, and Human Rights* (New Haven, Conn., 1982); Owen M. Fiss, "Foreword: The Forms of Justice," *Harvard Law Review* 93 (1979): 1–58, at 10.

44. Mark V. Tushnet, "The Dilemmas of Liberal Constitutionalism," *Ohio State Law Journal* 42 (1981): 411–26; Richard A. Parker, "The Past of Constitutional Theory—and Its Future," *Ohio State Law Journal* 42 (1981): 223–60.

45. Richard Delgado, "The Ethereal Scholar: Does Critical Legal Studies Have What Minorities Want?" *Harvard Civil Rights–Civil Liberties Law Review* 22 (1987): 311–22; Mari J. Matsuda, "Accent, Antidiscrimination Law, and a Jurisprudence for the Last Reconstruction," *Yale Law Journal* 100 (1991): 1329–1407.

46. Robin West, "Equality Theory, Marital Rape, and the Promise of the Fourteenth Amendment," *Florida Law Review* 42 (1990): 45–79; Christine A. Littleton, "Reconstructing Sexual Equality," *California Law Review* 75 (1987): 1279–1337.

47. 478 U.S. 186 (1986).

48. Philip B. Heymann and Douglas E. Barzelay, "The Forest and the Trees: *Roe v. Wade* and Its Critics," *Boston University Law Review* 53 (1973): 765–84; Michael J. Perry, "Abortion, the Public Morals, and the Police Power: The Ethical Function of Substantive Due Process," *U.C.L.A. Law Review* 23 (1976): 689–736. Perry has since changed his position; see Michael J. Perry, *Love and Power: The Role of Religion and Morality in American Politics* (New York, 1991).

49. John Hart Ely, "The Wages of Crying Wolf: A Comment on *Roe v. Wade*," *Yale Law Journal* 82 (1973): 920–49; Harry H. Wellington, "Common Law Rules and Constitutional Double Standards," *Yale Law Journal* 83 (1973): 223–312, at 297–311.

50. Tribe, *American Constitutional Law*, pp. 1425–29; Daniel O. Conkle, "The Second Death of Substantive Due Process," *Indiana Law Journal* 62 (1987): 215–22; Ali Kahn, "The Invasion of Sexual Privacy," *San Diego Law Review* 23 (1986): 957–78; Sylvia A. Law, "Homosexuality and the Social Meaning of Gender," *Wisconsin Law Review* (1988): 187–236; Frank I. Michelman, "Law's Republic," *Yale Law Journal* 97 (1988): 1493–1538; David A. J. Richards, "Constitutional Legitimacy and Constitutional Privacy," *New York University Law Review* 61 (1986): 800–862; Jeb Rubenfeld, "The Right of Privacy," *Harvard Law Review* 102 (1989): 737–807, at 799–802; Thomas B. Stoddard, "*Bowers v. Hardwick:* Precedent by Predilection," *University of Chicago Law Review* 54 (1987): 648–56; Norman Viera, "*Hardwick* and the Right of Privacy," *University of Chicago Law Review* 55 (1988): 1181–92; "The Supreme Court—1985 Term," *Harvard Law Review* 100 (1986): 100–305, at 210–20. See also Anne E. Goldstein, "History, Homosexuality, and Political Values: Searching for the Hidden Determinant of *Bowers v. Hardwick*," *Yale Law Journal* 97 (1988): 1073–1104, at 1103 (*Bowers* decision "mischaracteriz[es] history and misunderstand[s] homosexuality.") For a rare opposing viewpoint, see David Chang, "Conflict, Coherence, and Constitutional Intent," *Iowa Law Review* 72 (1987): 753–890, at 820–23.

51. E.g., Goldstein, "History, Homosexuality, and Political Values," pp. 1098–1103; Stoddard, "Precedent by Predilection," p. 655.

52. Law, "Homosexuality and the Social Meaning of Gender."

53. Sen. Exec. Rept. 100-7, 100th Cong., 1st sess., 1984, p. 211 (additional remarks of Senator Heflin).

54. Robert H. Bork, "The Constitution, Original Intent, and Economic Rights," *San Diego Law Review* 23 (1986): 823-32.

55. Sen. Exec. Rept. 100-7, 100th Cong., 1st sess., 1987, pp. 34-36 (contraception); pp. 45-49 (sex discrimination); pp. 131-32 (testimony of William J. Coleman, Jr., regarding abortion).

56. See, e.g., *New York Times*, 20 December 1987, p. E18; *Washington Post*, 12 November 1987, p. A37.

57. Richard A. Epstein, *Takings: Private Property and the Power of Eminent Domain* (Chicago, 1985); Richard A. Epstein, "Toward a Revitalization of the Contracts Clause," *University of Chicago Law Review* 51 (1984): 703-52.

58. Randy E. Barnett, "Reconceiving the Ninth Amendment," *Cornell Law Review* 74 (1988): 1-42; Randy E. Barnett, "Foreword: Judicial Conservatism v. Principled Judicial Activism," *Harvard Journal of Law and Public Policy* 10 (1987): 273-94.

59. Stephen Macedo, *The New Right v. the Constitution* (Washington, D.C., 1987); Stephen Macedo, "Majority Power, Moral Skepticism, and the New Right's Constitution," in *Economic Liberties and the Judiciary*, ed. James A. Dorn and Henry G. Manne (Fairfax, Va., 1987), pp. 111-37

60. Bernard H. Siegan, *Economic Liberties and the Constitution* (Chicago, 1980).

61. 403 U.S. 15 (1971).

62. Ibid., p. 25.

63. 468 U.S. 288 (1984).

64. Ibid., pp. 301-16 (Marshall, J., dissenting).

65. 491 U.S. 397 (1989).

66. Ibid., p. 414 (citations omitted).

67. Frank I. Michelman, "Saving Old Glory: On Constitutional Iconography," *Stanford Law Review* 42 (1990): 1337-64; Geoffrey R. Stone, "Flag Burning and the Constitution," *Iowa Law Review* (1989): 111-24.

68. Robert H. Bork, *The Tempting of America: The Political Seduction of the Law* (New York, 1990), pp. 127-28.

69. 112 S. Ct. 2538 (1992).

70. Ibid., pp. 2550-60 (White, J., concurring in the result); pp. 2660-61 (Blackmun, J., concurring in the result); pp. 2661-71 (Stevens, J., concurring in the result).

71. Ibid., p. 2547.

72. Marjorie Heins, "Banning Words: A Comment on 'Words That Wound,'" *Harvard Civil Rights–Civil Liberties Law Review* 18 (1983): 585-624; Nadine Strossen, "Regulating Racist Speech on Campus: A Modest Proposal," *Duke Law Journal* (1990): 484-573.

73. Charles R. Lawrence, "If He Hollers Let Him Go: Regulating Racist Speech on Campus," *Duke Law Journal* (1990): 431-83; Mari J. Matsuda, "Public Response to Racist Speech: Considering the Victim's Story," *Michigan Law Review* 87 (1989): 2320-81.

74. The conservative attack on political correctness is encapsulated in Dinesh D'Souza, *Illiberal Education: The Politics of Race and Sex on Campus* (New York, 1991).

75. This point is also made in Blackmun's concurrence in R.A.V. v. St Paul, 112 S. Ct. 2538 (1992) at 2561.

76. 431 U.S. 1 (1977).

77. 438 U.S. 234 (1978).

78. United States v. Central Eureka Mining Co., 357 U.S. 155, 168 (1958).

79. E.g., Goldblatt v. Hempstead, 369 U.S. 590 (1962); Berman v. Parker, 348 U.S. 26 (1954); United States v. Causby, 328 U.S. 256 (1946).

80. E.g., Loretto v. Teleprompter Manhattan CATV Corp., 458 U.S. 419 (1982); Kaiser Aetna v. United States, 444 U.S. 164 (1979).

81. For examples of the ongoing debate among academics, see Bruce A. Ackerman, *Private Property and the Constitution* (New Haven, Conn., 1977); Epstein, *Takings*; "Symposium: The Jurisprudence of Takings," *Columbia Law Review* 88 (1988): 1581–1795.

82. 438 U.S. 104 (1978).

83. 480 U.S. 470 (1987).

84. 483 U.S. 325 (1987).

85. 112 S. Ct. 2886 (1992).

86. Ibid., p. 2895 (emphasis in original).

87. Bork, *The Political Seduction of the Law*; Lino A. Graglia, "Judicial Activism: Even on the Right, It's Wrong," *Public Interest* 95 (1989): 57–74.

88. Ibid., pp. 126–28.

CHAPTER 2. ORIGINALISM AND ITS CRITICS

1. Raoul Berger, *Government by Judiciary: The Transformation of the Fourteenth Amendment* (Cambridge, Mass., 1977).

2. Robert H. Bork, *The Tempting of America: The Political Seduction of the Law* (New York, 1990).

3. See, for example, the essays collected in Gregory Leyh, ed., *Legal Hermeneutics: History, Theory, and Practice* (Chicago, 1992); Ronald Dworkin, "Law as Interpretation," *Texas Law Review* 60 (1982): 527–50; Robert H. Weisberg, "Text into Theory: A Literary Approach to the Constitution," *Georgia Law Review* 20 (1986): 939–94.

4. Richard Posner, "Law and Literature: A Puzzle Reargued," *Virginia Law Review* 72 (1986): 1351–92, at 1364–65.

5. 111 S. Ct. 1196 (1991).

6. Ibid., p. 1216 (Scalia, J., concurring in the result).

7. Metro Broadcasting, Inc. v. FCC, 497 U.S. 547, 631–38 (1990) (Scalia, J., joining dissent of Kennedy, J.); City of Richmond v. J. A. Croson Co., 488 U.S. 469, 520–28 (1989) (Scalia, J., concurring in the judgment).

8. 481 U.S. 69 (1987).

9. Ibid., pp. 96–97 (Scalia, J., concurring in part and concurring in the judgment in part).

10. Robert W. Bennett, "The Mission of Moral Reasoning in Constitutional Law," *Southern California Law Review* 58 (1985): 647–59, at 648.

11. See, for example, Perez v. United States, 402 U.S. 146 (1971); Katzenbach v. McClung, 379 U.S. 294 (1964).

12. Arguments similar to some of those in this section can be found in Gregory Bassham, *Original Intent and the Constitution: A Philosophical Study* (Berkeley, Calif., 1992); Richard S. Kay, "Adherence to the Original Intentions in Constitutional Adjudication: Three Objections and Responses," *Northwestern University Law Review* 82 (1988): 228–92; and Earl M. Maltz, "The Failure of Attacks on Constitutional Originalism," *Constitutional Commentary* 4 (1987): 43–56.

13. Paul Brest, "The Misconceived Quest for the Original Understanding," *Boston University Law Review* 60 (1980): 204–54.

14. Ibid., pp. 209–21.

15. Ibid., p. 221.

16. Ronald Dworkin, "The Forum of Principle," *New York University Law Review* 56 (1981): 469–518, at 482–97.

17. Ronald M. Dworkin, *Taking Rights Seriously* (Cambridge, Mass., 1977), pp. 133–37. Dworkin elaborates his anti-originalist argument further in Ronald M. Dworkin, *Law's Empire* (Cambridge, Mass., 1986), chaps. 6 and 7.

18. Mark v. Tushnet, "Following the Rules Laid Down: A Critique of Interpretivism and Neutral Principles," *Harvard Law Review* 96 (1983): 781–827.

19. This position is taken in Robert L. Clinton, *Marbury v. Madison and Judicial Review* (Lawrence, Kans., 1989), and William W. Crosskey, *Politics and the Constitution in the History of the United States*, 2 vols. (Chicago, 1953).

20. Among the authorities taking this view are Raoul Berger, *Congress v. the Supreme Court* (Cambridge, Mass., 1969); Edward S. Corwin, *The Doctrine of Judicial Review* (Princeton, N.J., 1914); Charles G. Haines, *The American Doctrine of Judicial Supremacy* (1932; repr. New York, 1973); Andrew C. McLaughlin, *A Constitutional History of the United States* (New York, 1935); and Charles Warren, *Congress, the Constitution, and the Supreme Court* (Boston, 1925).

21. Leonard W. Levy, *Original Intent and the Framers' Constitution* (New York, 1988), pp. 21–29; H. Jefferson Powell, "The Original Understanding of Original Intent," *Harvard Law Review* 98 (1985): 885–948.

22. "Essays of Brutus: No. 11" in Herbert J. Storing, ed., *The Complete Anti-Federalist*, 7 vols. (Chicago, 1981), 2: 419, 420–21, quoted in Powell, "Original Understanding," p. 908.

23. Letter to Spencer Roane, 2 September 1819, in *The Writings of James Madison*, ed. Gaillard Hunt, 9 vols. (New York, 1900–1910), 8: 447, 450, quoted in Levy, *Original Intent*, p. 21, and Powell, "Original Understanding," p. 941.

24. Ibid.

25. Powell, "Original Understanding," p. 941.

26. Forrest McDonald, *Novus Ordo Seclorum: The Intellectual Origins of the Constitution* (Lawrence, Kans., 1985), pp. 205–9.

27. "Essays of Brutus: No. 12," in Storing, *The Complete Anti-Federalist*, 2: 425, quoted in Powell, "Original Understanding," p. 908 n. 124.

28. 17 U.S. (4 Wheat.) 316 (1819).

29. Ibid., p. 407.

30. Ibid., p. 419.

31. Ibid., p. 407.

32. 3 Va. 20 (1790).

33. Ibid., p. 40 (opinion of Judge Roane).

34. Ibid., p. 61 (opinion of Judge Tyler).

35. Ibid., p. 38 (opinion of Judge Roane).

36. Levy, *Original Intent*, pp. 17–20; Powell, "Original Understanding," pp. 906–7.

37. Powell, "Original Understanding," pp. 896–97.

38. Sir William Blackstone, *Commentaries on the Laws of England*, 4 vols. (London, 1766–1769), 1:59–61.

39. St. George Tucker, *Blackstone's Commentaries. With Notes of Reference to the Constitution and Laws of the Federal Government of the United States and of the Commonwealth of Virginia*, 5 vols. (Philadelphia, 1803), vol. 1, app. p. 151.

40. Philip B. Kurland and Ralph Lerner, eds., *The Founders Constitution*, 5 vols. (Chicago, 1987), 1:187.

41. Alexander Hamilton, John Jay, and James Madison, *The Federalist Papers*, ed. Jacob E. Cooke (Middletown, Conn., 1961), no. 40, p. 264. All subsequent citations refer to this edition.

42. Gordon S. Wood, *The Creation of the American Republic, 1776-1787* (New York, 1969), pp. 532-36.

43. *Federalist No. 39*, p. 254.

44. *Federalist No. 78*, p. 525.

45. A similar argument is made in Laurence G. Sager, "Rights Skepticism and Process-based Responses," *New York University Law Review* 56 (1981): 417-45, at 443-44.

46. Powell, "Original Understanding," pp. 904-5.

47. Jonathan Elliot, ed., *The Debates, Resolutions, and Other Proceedings, in Convention, on the Adoption of the Federal Constitution* (Philadelphia, 1827-1830), 3:286, quoted in Powell, "Original Understanding," p. 929; Wood, *Creation of the American Republic*, pp. 532-36.

48. *Federalist No. 39*, p. 254 (emphasis in original).

49. McDonald, *Novus Ordo Seclorum*, pp. 280-81. Powell argues that *Federalist No. 15* conclusively rejects the compact theory; Powell, "Original Understanding," p. 904 n. 98. There, however, Hamilton was not discussing the theoretical source of legitimacy of the new Constitution but the practical problems faced by the federal government under the Articles of Confederation.

50. Among the more lucid contemporary discussions of the theory of state sovereignty are the arguments of counsel in State v. Hunt, 9 So. Car. 1, 1-210 (1834), and John C. Calhoun's famous "Fort Hill Address," in *Papers of John C. Calhoun*, ed. Clyde N. Wilson, 18 vols. (Columbia, S.C., 1959-1988), 11:413-40. Perceptive modern summaries and analysis include William W. Freehling, *Prelude to Civil War: The Nullification Crisis in South Carolina* (New York, 1966), chap. 5; and Albert Bestor, "State Sovereignty and Slavery: A Reinterpretation of Proslavery Constitutional Doctrine, 1846-1860," *Journal of the Illinois State Historical Society* 54 (1961): 148.

51. The arguments against the legitimacy of the Constitution are discussed cogently in Richard S. Kay, "The Illegality of the Constitution," *Constitutional Commentary* 4 (1987): 57-80.

52. The wide variety of ideological and practical imperatives that interacted in the framing of the Constitution is described in McDonald, *Novus Ordo Seclorum*, chap. 6.

53. *Federalist No. 45* (Madison), p. 313.

54. *Federalist No. 22* (Hamilton), pp. 135-36; Albert S. Abel, "The Commerce Clause in the Constitutional Convention and in Contemporary Comment," *Minnesota Law Review* 25 (1941): 432-99, at 443-46.

55. For example, see "Essays of an Old Whig: No. 6," in Storing, *The Complete Anti-Federalist*, 3:39; "Notes of Samuel Chase," ibid., 5:79; "Essays by a Georgian," ibid., 5:130.

56. Abel, "The Commerce Clause in the Constitutional Convention," pp. 451-53.

CHAPTER 3. ORIGINALISM AND LIMITS ON FEDERAL POWER

1. 22 U.S. (9 Wheat.) 1 (1824).

2. 17 U.S. (4 Wheat.) 316 (1819).

3. Dred Scott v. Sandford, 60 U.S. (19 How.) 393 (1857).

4. *Congressional Globe*, 39th Cong., 1st sess., 1866, p. 1292 (remarks of Congressman Bingham).

5. 109 U.S. 3 (1883).

6. 156 U.S. 1 (1895).

7. 247 U.S. 251 (1918).

8. 295 U.S. 495 (1935).

9. 298 U.S. 238 (1936).

10. Oregon v. Mitchell, 400 U.S. 112 (1970).

11. 426 U.S. 833 (1976).

12. 392 U.S. 183 (1968).

13. 421 U.S. 542 (1975).

14. Usery, 426 U.S. at 845.

15. Ibid., p. 856 (Blackmun, J., concurring).

16. 460 U.S. 226 (1983).

17. 456 U.S. 742 (1982).

18. 469 U.S. 528 (1985).

19. Ibid., p. 531.

20. 112 S. Ct. 2408 (1992).

21. Ibid., p. 2423 (citations omitted).

22. Examples of such characterizations include John E. Nowak, Ronald D. Rotunda, and Nelson Young, *Constitutional Law*, 2d ed. (St. Paul, Minn., 1982), p. 171; Ronald D. Rotunda, "The Doctrine of Constitutional Preemption and Other Limitations on Tenth Amendment Restrictions," *University of Pennsylvania Law Review* 132 (1984): 289–326, at 291 and n. 9; and Richard B. Stewart, "Problems of Federalism in National Environmental Policy," *Yale Law Journal* 86 (1977): 1196–1272, at 1269–72.

23. Perez v. United States, 402 U.S. 146, 157–58 (1971) (Stewart, J., dissenting).

24. FERC, 456 U.S. at 775–97 (O'Connor, J., dissenting in part); ibid., pp. 771–75 (Powell, J., dissenting in part).

25. Ibid., p. 775 (O'Connor, J., dissenting in part).

26. Ibid., pp. 775–776 n. 1.

27. Ibid.

28. 452 U.S. 264 (1981).

29. Ibid., p. 305 (Burger, C.J., concurring); ibid., pp. 305–7 (Powell, J., concurring); ibid., pp. 307–13 (Rehnquist, J., concurring in the judgment).

30. Ibid., p. 305 (Powell, J., concurring).

31. 455 U.S. 678 (1982).

32. New York, 112 S. Ct. at 2425–27.

33. Bruce A. Ackerman, *We the People* (Cambridge, Mass., 1991), vol. 1, chap. 2.

34. Suzanna Sherry, "The Ghost of Liberalism Past," *Harvard Law Review* 105 (1991): 918–34.

35. *Federalist No. 40*, pp. 263–67.

36. Ackerman, *We the People*, pp. 251–55.

37. Ibid., pp. 181–91.

38. *Federalist No. 78*, p. 525.

39. Ibid., pp. 527–28.

40. Ackerman, *We the People*, p. 193.

41. Sherry, "The Ghost of Liberalism Past," p. 927.

42. Akhil R. Amar, "Philadelphia Revisited: Amending the Constitution outside Article V," *University of Chicago Law Review* 55 (1988): 1043–1104, at 1047–60.

43. Walter J. Suthon, Jr., "The Dubious Origin of the Fourteenth Amendment," *Tulane Law Review* 28 (1953): 22–44, makes the case against the legitimacy of the Fourteenth Amendment.

44. Ackerman, *We the People*, chap. 2.

45. Jesse H. Choper, *Judicial Review and the National Political Process* (Chicago, 1980); Herbert Wechsler, "The Political Safeguards of Federalism: The Role of the States in the Composition and Selection of the National Government," *Columbia Law Review* 54 (1954): 543–60.

46. Garcia, 469 U.S. at 550–54.

47. Alexander M. Bickel, "Foreword: The Passive Virtues," *Harvard Law Review* 75 (1961): 40–79, makes the best argument in favor of prudential considerations.

48. Marbury v. Madison, 5 U.S. (1 Cranch.) 137 (1803). The development of the political question doctrine is discussed in detail in Louis Henkin, "Is There a 'Political Question' Doctrine?" *Yale Law Journal* 85 (1976): 597–625.

49. Laurence H. Tribe, *American Constitutional Law*, 2d ed. (New York, 1988), p. 388.

50. A similar, more extended argument can be found in Lewis B. Kaden, "Politics, Money, and State Sovereignty: The Judicial Role," *Columbia Law Review* 79 (1979): 847–97.

51. For examples of such conflation, see Choper, *Judicial Review and the Political Process*; Kaden, "Politics, Money, and State Sovereignty," pp. 855–57.

52. *Federalist No. 84*, p. 579.

53. Gordon S. Wood, *The Creation of the American Republic, 1776–1787* (New York, 1969), pp. 538–40.

54. The evolution of the Tenth Amendment is described in Charles A. Lofgren, "The Origins of the Tenth Amendment," in *"Government from Reflection and Choice": Constitutional Essays on War, Foreign Relations, and Federalism*, by Charles A. Lofgren (New York, 1986), pp. 70–115.

55. Quoted in ibid., p. 103.

56. Ibid.

57. McDonald, *Novus Ordo Seclorum*, pp. 10–36, 63–66; Jennifer Nedelsky, *Private Property and the Limits of American Constitutionalism: The Madisonian Framework and Its Legacy* (Chicago, 1990).

58. Wood, *Creation of the American Republic*, pp. 403–9.

59. *Federalist Nos. 45, 46,* and 51.

60. *Federalist No. 78*, p. 526.

61. Quoted in Wood, *Creation of the American Republic*, p. 538.

CHAPTER 4. DEMOCRATIC THEORY, LEGITIMACY, AND NONORIGINALIST INTERVENTIONISM

1. William H. Rehnquist, "The Notion of a Living Constitution," *Texas Law Review* 54 (1976): 693–706, at 705. To the same effect, see Robert H. Bork, "Neutral Principles and Some First Amendment Problems," *Indiana Law Journal* 47 (1971): 1–35, at 2–4; Henry P. Monaghan, "Our Perfect Constitution," *New York University Law Review* 56 (1981): 353–96, at pp. 371–72.

2. E.g., John Hart Ely, *Democracy and Distrust: A Theory of Judicial Review*

(Cambridge, Mass., 1980); Frank I. Michelman, "Law's Republic," *Yale Law Journal* 97 (1988): 1493–1538.

3. Ely, *Democracy and Distrust.*

4. 426 U.S. 833 (1976), overruled, Garcia v. San Antonio Metropolitan Transit Authority, 469 U.S. 528 (1985).

5. 447 U.S. 74 (1980).

6. 391 U.S. 308 (1968).

7. See Marsh v. Alabama, 326 U.S. 501 (1946).

8. 407 U.S. 551 (1972).

9. 424 U.S. 507 (1976).

10. Robins v. Pruneyard Shopping Center, 23 Cal. 3d 899, 592 P.2d 341, 153 Cal. Rptr. 854 (1979), affirmed, 447 U.S. 74 (1980).

11. 447 U.S. at 85, quoting Nebbia v. New York, 291 U.S. 502, 525 (1934).

12. 377 U.S. 533 (1964).

13. 383 U.S. 663 (1966).

14. Raoul Berger, *Government by Judiciary: The Transformation of the Fourteenth Amendment* (Cambridge, Mass., 1977), pp. 363–72.

15. Robert H. Bork, *The Tempting of America: The Political Seduction of the Law* (New York, 1990), pp. 143–55.

16. Herbert Wechsler, "Toward Neutral Principles of Constitutional Law," *Harvard Law Review* 73 (1959): 1–35.

17. R. Kent Greenawalt, "The Enduring Significance of Neutral Principles," *Columbia Law Review* 78 (1978): 982–1021.

18. Wechsler, "Neutral Principles," p. 19.

CHAPTER 5. NEO-ORIGINALIST DEFENSES
OF JUDICIAL INTERVENTIONISM

1. Richard A. Epstein, *Takings: Private Property and the Power of Eminent Domain* (Chicago, 1985).

2. Richard A. Epstein, "Toward a Revitalization of the Contracts Clause," *University of Chicago Law Review* 51 (1984): 703–52.

3. Harold M. Hyman and William M. Wiecek, *Equal Justice under Law: Constitutional Development 1835–1875* (New York, 1982), chap. 11.

4. Much of the literature dealing with the Ninth Amendment is collected in Randy E. Barnett, ed., *The Rights Retained by the People: The History and Meaning of the Ninth Amendment* (Fairfax, Va., 1989).

5. 381 U.S. 479, 488–93, 496 (1965) (Goldberg, J., concurring).

6. Randy E. Barnett, "A Ninth Amendment for Today's Constitution," *Valparaiso University Law Review* 26 (1991): 419–35; Randy E. Barnett, "Reconceiving the Ninth Amendment," *Cornell Law Review* 74 (1988): 1–42; Randy E. Barnett, "Two Conceptions of the Ninth Amendment," *Harvard Journal of Law and Public Policy* 12 (1989): 29–41.

7. John Hart Ely, *Democracy and Distrust: A Theory of Judicial Review* (Cambridge, Mass., 1980), pp. 33–40.

8. Leonard W. Levy, *Original Intent and the Framers' Constitution* (New York, 1988), chap. 13.

9. Laurence H. Tribe and Michael C. Dorf, *On Reading the Constitution* (Cambridge, Mass., 1991).

10. Raoul Berger, "The Ninth Amendment," *Cornell Law Review* 61 (1980): 1–26.

11. Russell L. Caplan, "The History and Meaning of the Ninth Amendment," *Virginia Law Review* 69 (1983): 223–68.

12. Thomas B. McAffee, "The Bill of Rights, Social Contract Theory, and the Rights 'Retained' by the People," *Southern University Law Review* 16 (1992): 267–305; Thomas B. McAffee, "The Original Meaning of the Ninth Amendment," *Columbia Law Review* 90 (1990): 1215–1320; Thomas B. McAffee, "Prolegomena to a Meaningful Debate of the 'Unwritten Constitution' Thesis," *University of Cincinnati Law Review* 61 (1992): 107–70.

13. James H. Hutson, "The Bill of Rights and the American Revolutionary Experience," in *A Culture of Rights: The Bill of Rights in Philosophy, Politics, and Law—1791 and 1991,* ed. Michael J. Lacey and Kned Haakonssen (New York, 1991), pp. 91–95.

14. Thomas C. Grey, "Origins of the Unwritten Constitution: Fundamental Law in American Revolutionary Thought," *Stanford Law Review* 30 (1978): 843–894, at 854–56; Suzanna Sherry, "The Founders' Unwritten Constitution," *University of Chicago Law Review* 54 (1987): 1127–77; Suzanna Sherry, "Natural Law in the States," *University of Cincinnati Law Review* 61 (1992): 171–222; Suzanna Sherry, "The Ninth Amendment: Righting an Unwritten Constitution," *Chicago-Kent Law Review* 64 (1988): 1001–14.

15. For differing perspectives on the framers' views of the role of natural law in the governing process, see, for example, Terry Brennan, "Natural Rights and the Constitution: The Original 'Original Intent,'" *Harvard Journal of Law and Public Policy* 15 (1992): 965–1029; Philip A. Hamburger, "Natural Rights, Natural Law, and American Constitutions," *Yale Law Journal* 102 (1993): 907–60; Helen K. Michael, "The Role of Natural Law in Early American Constitutionalism: Did the Founders Contemplate Judicial Enforcement of 'Unwritten' Constitutional Rights?" *North Carolina Law Review* 69 (1991): 421–90.

16. 3 U.S. (3 Dall.) 386 (1794).

17. Ibid., pp. 387–88 (opinion of Chase, J.).

18. Ibid., p. 397 (opinion of Patterson, J.).

19. Ibid., p. 399 (opinion of Iredell, J.).

20. Sources cited in Laurence H. Tribe, *American Constitutional Law*, 2d ed. (Mineola, N.Y., 1988), p. 776 n. 14.

21. Laurence G. Sager, "You Can Raise the First, Hide behind the Fourth, and Plead the Fifth, But What on Earth Can You Do with the Ninth Amendment?" *Chicago-Kent Law Review* 64 (1988): 239–64, at 253.

22. My views on the basic issue of incorporation can be found in Earl M. Maltz, *Civil Rights, the Constitution, and Congress, 1863–1869* (Lawrence, Kans., 1990), pp. 113–18.

23. Sager, "You Can Raise the First," pp. 253–54.

24. *Congressional Globe*, 39th Cong., 1st sess., 1866, p. 2765 (Howard); ibid., 42d Cong., 1st sess., 1872, app. 84 (Bingham).

25. See, for example, Tribe, *American Constitutional Law*, p. 1514; Ely, *Democracy and Distrust*, pp. 11–41; Robert Sedler, "The Legitimacy Debate in Constitutional Theory: An Assessment and a Different Perspective," *Ohio State Law Journal* 44 (1983): 93–137, at 126–37.

26. Tribe, *American Constitutional Law*, pp. 1514–17.

27. The analysis that follows is a greatly condensed version of the argument in Maltz, *Civil Rights, the Constitution, and Congress*.

28. *Congressional Globe*, 39th Cong., 1st sess., 1866, p. 2765; see also p. 1034 (remarks of Congressman Bingham).

29. E.g., Corfield v. Coryell, 6 F. Cas. 546, 551–52 (C.C.E.D. Pa. 1823); Abbot v. Bayley, 23 Mass. (6 Pick.) 89, 92 (1827); Campbell v. Morris, 3 H. & Mch. 553, 554 (Md. 1797).

30. E.g., Dred Scott v. Sandford, 60 U.S. (19 How.) 393, 417 (1857) (right to free speech). Corfield v. Coryell, 6 F. Cas. 546, 551 (1823), also suggests that the right to vote is protected by the comity clause. This suggestion was clearly an aberration— e.g., Campbell v. Morris, 3 H. & Mch. 553, 554 (Md. 1797)—and was viewed as such by the drafters of the Fourteenth Amendment. See *Congressional Globe*, 39th Cong., 1st sess., p. 2766 (remarks of Senator Howard); and p. 2542 (remarks of Congressman Bingham).

31. The nineteenth-century understanding of the concept of due process of law is described in detail in Thomas M. Cooley, *A Treatise on the Constitutional Limitations Which Rest upon the Legislative Power* (Boston, 1868; repr. New York, 1972); Rodney L. Mott, *Due Process of Law: A Historical and Analytical Treatise of the Principles and Methods Followed by the Courts in the Application of the Concept of the "Law of the Land"* (Indianapolis, 1926); Howard J. Graham, *Everyman's Constitution* (Madison, Wis., 1968), pp. 242–65 (1968); Michael Les Benedict, "Laissez-Faire and Liberty: A Reevaluation of the Origins and Meaning of Laissez-Faire Constitutionalism," *Law and History Review* 3 (1985): 293–322; Edward S. Corwin, "The Doctrine of Due Process of Law before the Civil War," *Harvard Law Review* 24 (1911): 366–479; and Lowell J. Howe, "The Meaning of 'Due Process of Law' prior to the Adoption of the Fourteenth Amendment," *California Law Review* 18 (1930): 583–610.

32. This point is discussed in greater detail in Earl M. Maltz, "Fourteenth Amendment Concepts in the Antebellum Era," *American Journal of Legal History* 32 (1988): 305–46.

33. E.g., Corfield v. Coryell, 6 F. Cas. 546, 551–52 (C.C.E.D. Pa. 1823); Campbell v. Morris, 3 H. & Mch. 553, 554 (Md. 1797).

34. James Kent, *Commentaries on American Law*, 10th ed., 4 vols. (Boston, 1860), 2:15, 331, 333–34.

35. Francis Lieber, *The Miscellaneous Writings of Francis Lieber* (Philadelphia, 1880), pp. 177–80.

36. 71 U.S. (4 Wall.) 281 (1866).

37. Ibid., p. 295.

38. See, for example, St. George Tucker, *Blackstone's Commentaries. With Notes of Reference to the Constitution and Laws of the Federal Government of the United States and of the Commonwealth of Virginia*, 5 vols. (Philadelphia, 1803), vol. 2, app. 77–79.

39. E.g., Roberts v. City of Boston, 59 Mass. (5 Cush.) 198, 206 (1849).

40. 59 Mass. at 206 (emphasis added).

41. Judith A. Baer, *Equality under the Constitution: Reclaiming the Fourteenth Amendment* (Ithaca, N.Y., 1983), p. 77; Hyman and Wiecek, *Equal Justice under Law*, pp. 95–96; Leonard Levy, *The Law of the Commonwealth and Chief Justice Shaw* (Cambridge, Mass., 1957), pp. 108–17.

42. Maltz, "Fourteenth Amendment Concepts," pp. 329–34.

43. Eric Foner, *Free Soil, Free Labor, Free Men* (New York, 1970), pp. 288–90; Robert W. Johannsen, ed., *The Lincoln-Douglas Debates of 1858* (New York, 1965), pp. 52–53.

44. Maltz, "Fourteenth Amendment Concepts," pp. 326–28.

45. Ibid., p. 329.

46. Jacobus tenBroek, *The Antislavery Origins of the Fourteenth Amendment* (Berkeley, Calif., 1951).

47. Robert J. Kaczorowski, "Revolutionary Constitutionalism in the Era of the Civil War and Reconstruction," *New York University Law Review* 61 (1986): 863–940.

48. Hyman and Wiecek, *Equal Justice under Law*, chap. 11.

49. *Congressional Globe*, 39th Cong., 1st sess., 1866. pp. 1366–67

50. See, for example, ibid., p. 1082 (remarks of Senator Stewart) and pp. 1082, 1087 (remarks of Congressman Davis).

51. Ibid., 40th Cong., 3d sess., 1869, p. 1041.

52. The political context of the debate over the Fourteenth Amendment is discussed in detail in Michael Les Benedict, *A Compromise of Principle: Congressional Republicans and Reconstruction 1863–1869* (New York, 1974); Joseph B. James, *The Framing of the Fourteenth Amendment* (Urbana, Ill., 1956); and Eric McKitrick, *Andrew Johnson and Reconstruction* (Chicago, 1960).

53. *Congressional Globe*, 39th Cong., 1st sess., 1866, p. 1292.

54. 100 U.S. 339, 345 (1879).

55. Cass R. Sunstein, "Interest Groups in American Public Law," *Stanford Law Review* 38 (1985): 29–87; Cass R. Sunstein, "Beyond the Republican Revival," *Yale Law Journal* 97 (1988): 1539–90. The historical accuracy of Sunstein's description of classical republicanism is questioned convincingly in Linda K. Kerber, "Making Republicanism Useful," *Yale Law Journal* 97 (1988): 1663–72, and Thomas L. Pangle, "Comments on Cass Sunstein's 'Republicanism and the Preference Problem,'" *Chicago-Kent Law Review* 66 (1990): 205–12.

56. Sunstein, "Interest Groups," p. 79.

57. Ibid., pp. 69–72.

58. Ibid. In recent years, the appeal to classical republicanism has become an increasingly important theme in the literature defending left/center interventionism. For other prominent examples, see Frank I. Michelman, "The Supreme Court, 1985 Term—Foreword: Traces of Self-Government," *Harvard Law Review* 100 (1986): 4–77; "Symposium: The Republican Civic Tradition," *Yale Law Journal* 97 (1988): 1493–1724. For a critique, see Richard H. Fallon, Jr., "What Is Republicanism, and Is It Worth Reviving," *Harvard Law Review* 102 (1989): 1695–1735.

59. David A. J. Richards, *Toleration and the Constitution* (New York, 1986).

60. David A. J. Richards, *Foundations of American Constitutionalism* (New York, 1989), p. 216.

61. E.g., Tribe, *American Constitutional Law*, p. 1514; Sedler, "The Legitimacy Debate in Constitutional Theory," pp. 126–37.

62. E.g., Immigration and Naturalization Service v. Cardoza-Fonesca, 480 U.S. 421 (1987); Church of the Holy Trinity v. United States, 143 U.S. 457 (1892). In recent years, this view has come under attack from a variety of different perspectives. See, e.g., Green v. Bock Laundry Machinery Co., 490 U.S. 504 (1988) (Scalia, J., concurring) (focus on plain meaning of statutory language; T. Alexander Aleinikoff, "Updating Statutory Interpretation," *Michigan Law Review* 87 (1988): 20–66; William N. Eskridge, "Dynamic Statutory Interpretation," *University of Pennsylvania Law Review* 135 (1987): 1479–1556; William N. Eskridge, "Gadamer/Statutory Interpretation," *Columbia Law Review* 90 (1990): 609–81. The traditional approach is defended in Earl M. Maltz, "Statutory Interpretation and Legislative Power: The Case for a Modified Intentionalist Approach," *Tulane Law Review* 63 (1988): 1–28;

and Richard Posner, "Legal Formalism, Legal Realism, and the Interpretation of Statutes and the Constitution," *Case Western Law Review* 37 (1986–87): 179–217.

63. 42 U.S.C. secs. 2000e–2000e-17 (1981).

64. E.g., Espinoza v. Farah Manufacturing Co., 414 U.S. 86 (1973) (discrimination against aliens not prohibited by statutory prohibition against discrimination on the basis of national origin).

65. U.S. Constitution, Article IV, section 4.

66. Ibid., Article I, section 2, clause 1.

67. *Federalist No. 62* (Madison), pp. 416–17.

68. E.g., *Federalist No. 54* (Madison).

69. For an excellent account of the maneuvering that produced section two, see Benedict, *A Compromise of Principle*, pp. 147–50.

70. U.S. Constitution, Amendment 15.

71. Ibid., Amendment 19.

72. Ibid., Amendment 24.

73. Ibid., Amendment 26.

74. Ibid., Amendment 17.

75. E.g., Voting Rights Act of 1965, 42 U.S.C. sec. 1973 (applying new federal standards to voter qualifications).

76. E.g., Wesberry v. Sanders, 376 U.S. 1 (1964) (principle of one person, one vote).

77. In-depth analyses of the various forces that shaped the Constitution can be found in Forrest McDonald, *Novus Ordo Seclorum: The Intellectual Origins of the Constitution* (Lawrence, Kans., 1985), and Gordon S. Wood, *The Creation of the American Republic, 1776–1787* (New York, 1969).

78. *Federalist No. 35* (Madison), p. 233.

79. Ibid., p. 233.

80. Ibid., p. 237.

81. Ibid.

82. Ibid., p. 238.

83. *Federalist No. 39*, p. 253.

84. *Federalist No. 62*, p. 416.

85. Ibid., pp. 416–17.

86. U.S. Constitution, Article IV, section 3.

87. *Federalist No. 42* (Madison), p. 282.

88. Ibid., p. 281.

89. *Federalist No. 54* (Madison).

90. *Federalist No. 41*, p. 268.

91. *Federalist No.84*, pp. 579–80.

92. Akhil R. Amar, "The Bill of Rights as a Constitution," *Yale Law Journal* 100 (1991): 1131–1210, provides an excellent discussion of the place of the Bill of Rights in the constitutional scheme.

93. The basic approaches of the theorists who take such positions are outlined in David A. Strauss, "Afterword: The Role of a Bill of Rights," *University of Chicago Law Review* 59 (1992): 539–66, at 548–59.

94. Ronald M. Dworkin, "Unenumerated Rights: Whether and How *Roe* Should Be Overruled," *University of Chicago Law Review* 59 (1992): 381–432, at 387.

95. Ibid., p. 382.

96. 381 U.S. 479 (1965).

97. The complex congressional deliberations that produced the final form of the

Bill of Rights are compiled in Bernard Schwartz, ed., *The Bill of Rights: A Documentary History*, 2 vols. (New York, 1971), vol. 2.

98. The drafting of the Reconstruction amendments is analyzed in much greater detail in Maltz, *Civil Rights, the Constitution, and Congress*.

99. See, for example, G. Sidney Buchanan, *The Quest for Freedom: A Legal History of the Thirteenth Amendment* (Houston, 1976); Hyman and Wiecek, *Equal Justice under Law*, chap. 11; tenBroek, *Antislavery Origins of the Fourteenth Amendment*.

100. See *Congressional Globe*, 38th Cong., 1st sess., 1864, p. 1488 (remarks of Senator Howard, criticizing Sumner language).

101. E.g., *Congressional Globe*, 39th Cong., 1st sess., 1866, p. 1292 (remarks of Congressman Bingham, explaining purpose for proposing amendment); and p. 2530 (remarks of Congressman Randall, opposing amendment).

102. E.g., ibid., pp. 2890–91 (remarks of Senator Howard); and p. 1292 (remarks of Congressman Bingham).

103. *Congressional Globe*, 39th Cong., 1st sess., 1866, p. 2446. In addition, see *Harper's Weekly*, 10 November 1866, p. 706; Open Letter from Carl Schurz to William Fessenden, *Cincinnati Commercial*, 18 May 1866, p. 2; *Springfield Republican*, 5 April 1866, p. 4; Eric Foner, *Reconstruction: America's Unfinished Revolution, 1863–1877* (New York, 1988), pp. 257–58; Harold M. Hyman, *A More Perfect Union: The Impact of the Civil War and Reconstruction on the Constitution* (New York, 1973), pp. 300–301, 393–96; William E. Nelson, *The Fourteenth Amendment: From Political Principle to Judicial Doctrine* (Cambridge, Mass., 1988).

104. Benjamin B. Kendrick, *The Journal of the Joint Committee on Reconstruction, 39th Congress, 1865–67* (New York, 1914), p. 62.

105. *Congressional Globe*, 39th Cong., 1st sess., 1866, p. 1292.

106. Ibid., p. 1087.

107. Ibid., p. 1082.

108. Ibid., p. 1095 (by implication).

109. Ibid., pp. 1063–64 (remarks of Congressman Hale). To the same effect, see *Springfield Republican*, 26 January 1866, p. 2.

110. *Congressional Globe*, 39th Cong., 1st sess., 1866, p. 2542.

111. *Report of the Joint Committee on Reconstruction*, 39th Cong., 1st sess. (1866), p. 12.

CHAPTER 6. FUNCTIONAL DEFENSES OF NONORIGINALIST INTERVENTIONISM

1. This point is central to Philip Bobbitt, *Constitutional Fate: A Theory of the Constitution* (New York, 1982), and Philip Bobbitt, *Constitutional Interpretation* (Cambridge, Mass., 1991).

2. 491 U.S. 110 (1989).

3. Ibid., pp. 113–32 (opinion of Scalia, J.).

4. Ibid., p. 123.

5. Ibid., p. 124.

6. Ibid., p. 125.

7. Ibid., p. 127.

8. Ibid., p. 128.

9. Ibid., pp. 136–57 (Brennan, J., dissenting).

10. Ibid., p. 141.

11. Ibid.

12. 438 U.S. 265 (1976).

13. 476 U.S. 267 (1986).

14. 488 U.S. 469 (1989).

15. David A. J. Richards, *Toleration and the Constitution* (New York, 1986).

16. Sylvia A. Law, "Homosexuality and the Social Meaning of Gender," *Wisconsin Law Review* (1988): 187–236; Sylvia A. Law, "Rethinking Sex and the Constitution," *University of Pennsylvania Law Review* 132 (1984): 955–1040.

17. Richard A. Epstein, *Takings: Private Property and the Power of Eminent Domain* (Chicago, 1985).

18. Leonard W. Levy, *Original Intent and the Framers' Constitution* (New York, 1988).

19. Labine v. Vincent, 401 U.S. 532 (1971).

20. Ibid., pp. 541–59 (Brennan, J., dissenting).

21. Ibid., pp. 552–53.

22. Ibid., p. 557.

23. Ibid., p. 541.

24. Robert A. Burt, "The Constitution of the Family," in *Supreme Court Review: 1979*, ed. Philip B. Kurland and Gerhard Casper (Chicago, 1980), pp. 329–95, at 388–91.

25. 431 U.S. 494 (1977) at 531–41 (Stewart, J., dissenting); ibid., pp. 541–52 (White, J., dissenting). Chief Justice Burger would have dismissed the challenge on procedural grounds; ibid., pp. 521–31 (Burger, C.J., dissenting).

26. 431 U.S. at 504–5 (opinion of Powell, J.) (footnote omitted).

27. While not joining the plurality opinion, Justice Stevens concluded that the ordinance was an unreasonable restraint on the grandmother's right to use her property. 431 U.S. at 513–21 (Stevens, J., concurring in the judgment).

28. 431 U.S. at 506 (opinion of Powell, J.).

29. This argument is derived from Earl M. Maltz, "Some New Thoughts on an Old Problem: The Role of the Intent of the Framers in Constitutional Theory," *Boston University Law Review* 63 (1983): 811–51.

30. Dred Scott v. Sandford, 60 U.S. (19 How.) 393 (1857).

31. Lochner v. New York, 198 U.S. 45 (1905).

32. Roe v. Wade, 410 U.S. 113 (1973).

33. Brown v. Board of Education of Topeka, 347 U.S. 483 (1954).

34. City of Richmond v. J. A. Croson Co., 488 U.S. 469 (1989).

35. Moore v. City of East Cleveland, 431 U.S. 494, 503–6 (1977) (opinion of Powell, J.); Poe v. Ullman, 367 U.S. 497, 542 (1961) (Harlan, J., dissenting); Ira C. Lupu, "Untangling the Strands of the Fourteenth Amendment," *Michigan Law Review* 77 (1979): 981–1077, at 1043–50.

36. Owen M. Fiss, "Foreword: The Forms of Justice," *Harvard Law Review* 93 (1979): 1–58, at 9–10.

37. Ronald M. Dworkin, "The Forum of Principle," *New York University Law Review* 56 (1981): 469–518, at 517–18.

38. For example, Erwin Chemerinsky, "Foreword: The Vanishing Constitution," *Harvard Law Review* 103 (1989): 43–104, at 84–85.

39. 198 U.S. 45 (1905).

40. John Hart Ely, *Democracy and Distrust: A Theory of Judicial Review* (Cambridge, Mass., 1980), pp. 56–58, suggests that this difficulty is insurmountable.

41. Mary Ann Glendon, *Rights Talk: The Impoverishment of Political Discourse* (New York, 1991).

42. The impact of these decisions is discussed in great detail in Jesse H. Choper, "Consequences of Supreme Court Decisions Upholding Constitutional Rights," *Michigan Law Review* 83 (1984): 1–212.

43. 347 U.S. 483 (1954).

44. Those views are discussed in detail in Maltz, "Some New Thoughts on an Old Problem," pp. 846–50.

45. 488 U.S. 469 (1989).

46. E.g., Morris Abram, "Affirmative Action: Fair Shakers and Social Engineers," *Harvard Law Review* 99 (1986): 1312–26.

47. E.g., Ronald M. Dworkin, *Taking Rights Seriously* (Cambridge, Mass., 1977), chap. 9; Laurence H. Tribe, "In What Vision of the Constitution Must the Law Be Color-Blind," *John Marshall Law Review* 20 (1986): 201–8.

48. 41 U.S. (16 Pet.) 539 (1842).

49. 60 U.S. (19 How.) 393 (1857).

50. 92 U.S. (2 Otto) 214 (1876).

51. 109 U.S. 3 (1883).

52. A similar argument is made in Girardeau A. Spann, *Race against the Court: The Supreme Court and Minorities in Contemporary America* (New York, 1993).

53. 402 U.S. 1 (1971).

54. 413 U.S. 189 (1973).

55. The internal struggles that shaped the Court's opinion in *Swann* are described in detail in Bernard Schwartz, *Swann's Way: The School Busing Case and the Supreme Court* (New York, 1971). The Court's reasoning and conclusions are criticized sharply in Lino A. Graglia, *Disaster by Decree: The Supreme Court Decisions on Race and the Schools* (Ithaca, N.Y., 1976), pp. 104–32.

56. *Keyes*, 413 U.S. at 254–65 (Rehnquist, J., dissenting); ibid., pp. 217–53 (Powell, J., concurring in part and dissenting in part).

57. 418 U.S. 718 (1974).

58. 443 U.S. 526 (1979).

59. 443 U.S. 449 (1979).

60. 493 U.S. 265 (1990).

61. 427 U.S. 424 (1976).

62. 498 U.S. 237 (1991).

63. 112 S. Ct. 1430 (1992).

64. 438 U.S. 265 (1978).

65. 448 U.S. 448 (1980).

66. Herman Belz, *Equality Transformed: A Quarter Century of Affirmative Action* (New Brunswick, N.J., 1991), chap. 3.

67. 476 U.S. 267 (1986). While the Bakke plan was found illegal, four of the justices relied solely on statutory grounds; Bakke, 438 U.S. at 408–21 (opinion of Stevens, J.).

68. 488 U.S. 469 (1989). See pp. 520–28 (Scalia, J., concurring in the result) and pp. 518–20 (Kennedy, J., concurring).

69. 497 U.S. 547 (1990).

70. 113 S. Ct. 2816 (1993).

71. The seminal article is Robert A. Dahl, "Decision-Maker in a Democracy: The Supreme Court as a National Policy-Maker," *Journal of Public Law* 6 (1957): 279–95.

72. Much of this section is taken from Earl M. Maltz, "The Supreme Court and the Quality of Political Dialogue," *Constitutional Commentary* 5 (1988): 375–91.

Similar arguments can be found in Mary Ann Glendon, *Abortion and Divorce in Western Law* (Cambridge, Mass., 1987), and Glendon, *Rights Talk*.

73. Alexander M. Bickel, *The Supreme Court and the Idea of Progress* (New Haven, Conn., 1970), p. 177.

74. Michael J. Perry, *The Constitution, the Courts, and Human Rights* (New Haven, Conn., 1982), p. 113.

75. E.g., Philip Bobbitt, *Constitutional Fate: A Theory of the Constitution* (Cambridge, Mass., 1982), pp. 182–83; Bruce A. Ackerman, "The Storrs Lectures: Discovering the Constitution," *Yale Law Journal* 93 (1984): 1013–72, at 1047–49; Wojiech Sadurski, "Conventional Morality and Judicial Standards," *Virginia Law Review* 73 (1987): 339–98, at 397. See generally, Robert F. Nagel, "Rationalism in Constitutional Law," *Constitutional Commentary* 4 (1987): 9–24, at 15.

76. 408 U.S. 238 (1971).

77. Ibid., pp. 257–306 (opinion of Brennan, J.); and pp. 314–74 (opinion of Marshall, J.).

78. Ibid., pp. 240–57 (opinion of Douglas, J.); pp. 306–10 (opinion of Stewart, J.); and pp. 310–14 (opinion of White, J.).

79. See, e.g., Roberts v. Louisiana, 462 U.S. 325 (1976); Woodson v. North Carolina, 428 U.S. 280 (1976); Jurek v. Texas, 428 U.S. 262 (1976); Gregg v. Georgia, 428 U.S. 242 (1976).

80. Abington School District v. Schempp, 374 U.S. 203 (1963); Engel v. Vitale, 370 U.S. 421 (1962).

81. Herbert Wechsler, "The Courts and the Constitution," *Columbia Law Review* 65 (1965): 1001–14, at 1002–3.

82. William N. Eskridge, "Overruling Supreme Court Statutory Interpretation Decisions," *Yale Law Journal* 101 (1991): 331–455, provides an in-depth analysis of the dialogue between the Court and Congress on issues of statutory interpretation.

83. 42 U.S.C. sec. 2000e (1976 ed.)

84. 429 U.S. 125 (1976).

85. Ibid., pp. 137–40.

86. 42 U.S.C. sec. 2000e(k) (1976 ed., supp. 5).

87. 462 U.S. 669 (1983).

88. Ibid., pp. 684–85.

89. See, e.g., 110 Cong. Rec. 7247 (1964).

90. 401 U.S. 424 (1971).

91. See Elizabeth Bartholet, "Application of Title VII to Jobs in High Places," *Harvard Law Review* 95 (1982): 945–1027, at 982–83; George A. Ruthergelen, "Title VII Class Actions," *University of Chicago Law Review* 47 (1980): 688–742, at 719 and nn. 186–87.

92. 490 U.S. 642 (1990).

93. Admittedly, the opportunity of the federal courts to participate in the dialogue over the proper shape of state law is more limited. The federal courts do, however, have some voice in this dialogue through the exercise of diversity jurisdiction. Moreover, a strong judicial voice is heard through the medium of the state courts.

94. "A Survey of the Present Statutory and Case Law on Abortion: The Contradictions and Problems," *University of Illinois Law Forum* (1972): 177–98, at 179–80 and nn. 27, 29.

95. See Ibid., p. 180 and n. 32.

96. For a detailed examination of the post-*Roe* activities of the prolife movement,

see Albert M. Pearson and Paul M. Kurtz, "The Abortion Controversy: A Study in Law and Politics," *Harvard Journal of Law and Public Policy* 8 (1985): 427–64.

97. See Roe v. Norton, 522 F. 2d 938 (2d Cir. 1975).

98. Public Law 96–123, sec. 109, 93 Stat. 926.

99. 488 U.S. 297 (1980).

100. Webster, 492 U.S. 490 (1989); Casey, 112 S. Ct. 2791 (1992).

101. John Hart Ely, *Democracy and Distrust: A Theory of Judicial Review* (Cambridge, Mass., 1980).

102. Ibid., p. 87.

103. Ibid., p. 88.

104. See, for example, Paul A. Brest, "The Substance of Process," *Ohio State Law Journal* 42 (1981): 131–42; Mark V. Tushnet, "The Dilemmas of Liberal Constitutionalism," *Ohio State Law Journal* 42 (1981): 411–24, at 424.

105. Adams to James Sullivan, in *The Works of John Adams*, ed. Charles Francis Adams, 10 vols. (Boston, 1850–1856), 9:375–78, quoted in Forrest McDonald, *Novus Ordo Seclorum: The Intellectual Origins of the Constitution* (Lawrence, Kans., 1985), p. 161.

106. McDonald, *Novus Ordo Seclorum*, p. 162.

107. Ibid., chap. 5; Gordon S. Wood, *The Creation of the American Republic, 1776–1787* (New York, 1969), chap. 12.

108. *Federalist No. 62* (Madison), p. 417.

109. Ely, *Democracy and Distrust*, p. 99.

110. For detailed discussions of the development of section two, see Michael Les Benedict, *A Compromise of Principle: Congressional Republicans and Reconstruction 1863–1869* (New York, 1974); Joseph B. James, *The Framing of the Fourteenth Amendment* (Urbana, Ill., 1956).

111. Extended discussions of the drafting of the Fifteenth Amendment include William Gillette, *The Right to Vote: Politics and the Passage of the Fifteenth Amendment* (Baltimore, 1965), and Earl M. Maltz, *Civil Rights, the Constitution, and Congress, 1863–1869* (Lawrence, Kans., 1990), pp. 142–56.

112. *Congressional Globe*, 40th Cong., 3d sess., 1869, app. 155.

113. Ibid., p. 1035.

114. Ibid., pp. 1040, 1044.

115. Ibid., p. 1037.

116. Ibid., p. 1038.

117. Ibid., p. 1426.

118. Ely, *Democracy and Distrust*, p. 99.

119. Ely, *Democracy and Distrust*, p. 161.

120. Gerald Rosberg, "Aliens and Equal Protection: Why Not the Right to Vote?" *Michigan Law Review* 75 (1977): 1092–1136.

121. Ely, *Democracy and Distrust*, pp. 162–70.

122. 411 U.S. 677 (1973).

123. Ibid., pp. 689–90.

124. U.S. Constitution, Article I, section 4, clause 1.

125. The distinction is drawn from Michael J. Perry, *The Constitution, the Court, and Human Rights* (New Haven, Conn., 1982).

SELECTED BIBLIOGRAPHY

A truly complete listing of the references that bear on the issues discussed in this book would almost certainly be longer than the book itself. Accordingly, this list of sources includes only works actually cited, together with other secondary sources that have had a particularly strong influence on my thinking.

CASES

United States Supreme Court

A. L. A. Schecter Poultry Corp. v. United States, 295 U.S. 495 (1935).
Abington School District v. Schempp, 374 U.S. 203 (1963).
Adamson v. California, 332 U.S. 46 (1947).
Allied Structural Steel v. Spannaus, 438 U.S. 234 (1978).
Berman v. Parker, 348 U.S. 26 (1954).
Board of Education of Oklahoma City Schools v. Dowell, 110 S. Ct. 630 (1991).
Bowers v. Hardwick, 478 U.S. 186 (1986).
Brown v. Board of Education of Topeka, 347 U.S. 483 (1954).
Calder v. Bull, 3 U.S. (3 Dall.) 386 (1794).
Carter v. Carter Coal Co., 298 U.S. 238 (1936).
Church of the Holy Trinity v. United States, 143 U.S. 457 (1892).
City of Akron v. Akron Center for Reproductive Health, 462 U.S. 416 (1983).
City of Richmond v. J. A. Croson Co., 488 U.S. 469 (1989).
Clark v. Community for Creative Non-Violence, 468 U.S. 288 (1984).
Civil Rights Cases, 109 U.S. 3 (1883).
Cohen v. California, 403 U.S. 15 (1971).
Columbus Board of Education v. Pennick, 443 U.S. 449 (1979).
Craig v. Boren, 429 U.S. 190 (1976).
CTS Corp. v. Dynamics Corp. of America, 481 U.S. 69 (1987).
Dandridge v. Williams, 397 U.S. 471 (1970).
Dayton Board of Education v. Brinkman, 443 U.S. 526 (1979).
Doe v. Bolton, 410 U.S. 179 (1973).
Dred Scott v. Sandford, 60 U.S. (19 How.) 393 (1857).
Duncan v. Louisiana, 391 U.S. 145 (1968).
E. C. Knight Co. v. United States, 156 U.S. 1 (1895).
EEOC v. Wyoming, 460 U.S. 226 (1983).
Engel v. Vitale, 370 U.S. 421 (1962).
Espinoza v. Farah Manufacturing Co., 414 U.S. 86 (1973).
Ex parte Milligan, 71 U.S. (4 Wall.) 281 (1866).
Ex parte Virginia, 100 U.S. 339 (1879).

Federal Energy Regulatory Commission v. Mississippi, 456 U.S. 742 (1982).
Food Employees Local 590 v. Logan Valley Plaza, Inc., 391 U.S. 308 (1968).
Freeman v. Pitts, 112 S. Ct. 1430 (1992).
Frontiero v. Richardson, 411 U.S. 677 (1973).
Fry v. United States, 421 U.S. 542 (1975).
Fullilove v. Klutznick, 448 U.S. 448 (1980).
Furman v. Georgia, 408 U.S. 238 (1971).
Garcia v. San Antonio Metropolitan Transit Authority, 469 U.S. 528 (1985).
General Electric Co. v. Gilbert, 429 U.S. 125 (1976).
Gibbons v. Ogden, 22 U.S. (9 Wheat.) 1 (1824).
Goldblatt v. Hempstead, 369 U.S. 590 (1962).
Graham v. Richardson, 403 U.S. 365 (1971).
Green v. Bock Laundry Machinery Co., 490 U.S. 504 (1988).
Gregg v. Georgia, 428 U.S. 242 (1976).
Griggs v. Duke Power Co., 401 U.S. 424 (1971).
Griswold v. Connecticut, 381 U.S. 479 (1965).
Hammer v. Dagenhart, 247 U.S. 251 (1918).
Harper v. Virginia Board of Elections, 383 U.S. 663 (1966).
Harris v. McRae, 448 U.S. 497 (1980).
Hodel v. Virginia Surface Mining and Reclamation Association, 452 U.S. 264 (1981).
Hudgens v. NLRB, 424 U.S. 507 (1976).
Immigration and Naturalization Service v. Cardoza-Fonesca, 480 U.S. 421 (1987).
Jurek v. Texas, 428 U.S. 262 (1976).
Kadrmas v. Dickinson Public Schools, 487 U.S. 450 (1988).
Kaiser Aetna v. United States, 444 U.S. 164 (1979).
Katzenbach v. McClung, 379 U.S. 294 (1964).
Keyes v. School District No. 1, 413 U.S. 189 (1973).
Keystone Bituminous Coal Association v. DeBenedictus, 480 U.S. 470 (1987).
Labine v. Vincent, 401 U.S. 532 (1971).
Lochner v. New York, 198 U.S. 45 (1905).
Lloyd Corp. v. Tanner, 407 U.S. 551 (1972).
Loretto v. Teleprompter Manhattan CATV Corp., 458 U.S. 419 (1982).
Lucas v. South Carolina Coastal Council, 112 S. Ct. 2886 (1992).
Mapp v. Ohio, 367 U.S. 643 (1961).
Marbury v. Madison, 5 U.S. (1 Cranch.) 137 (1803).
Marsh v. Alabama, 326 U.S. 501 (1946).
Maryland v. Wirtz, 392 U.S. 183 (1968).
McCulloch v. Maryland, 17 U.S. (4 Wheat.) 316 (1819).
Metro Broadcasting Corp. v. FCC, 497 U.S. 547 (1990).
Michael H. v. Gerald D., 491 U.S. 110 (1989).
Milliken v. Bradley, 418 U.S. 718 (1974).
Miranda v. Arizona, 384 U.S. 436 (1966).
Moore v. City of East Cleveland, 431 U.S. 494 (1977).
National League of Cities v. Usery, 426 U.S. 833 (1976).
Nebbia v. New York, 291 U.S. 502 (1934).
New York v. United States, 112 S. Ct. 2408 (1992).
Newport News Shipbuilding and Drydock Co. v. EEOC, 462 U.S. 669 (1983).
NLRB v. Jones & Laughlin Steel Co., 301 U.S. 1 (1937).
Nollan v. California Coastal Commission, 483 U.S. 325 (1987).
Oregon v. Mitchell, 400 U.S. 112 (1970).
Pasadena City Board of Education v. Spangler, 427 U.S. 424 (1976).

Penn Central Transportation Co. v. City of New York, 438 U.S. 104 (1978).
Perez v. United States, 402 U.S. 146 (1971).
Planned Parenthood of Southeastern Pennsylvania v. Casey, 112 S. Ct. 2791 (1992).
Plyler v. Doe, 457 U.S. 202 (1982).
Poe v. Ullman, 367 U.S. 497 (1961).
Pruneyard Shopping Center v. Robins, 447 U.S. 74 (1980).
Prigg v. Pennsylvania, 41 U.S. (16 Pet.) 539 (1842).
Railroad Retirement Board v. Alton Railroad Co., 295 U.S. 330 (1935).
R.A.V. v. St. Paul, 112 S. Ct. 2538 (1992).
Reynolds v. Sims, 377 U.S. 533 (1964).
Roberts v. Louisiana, 462 U.S. 325 (1976).
Roe v. Wade, 410 U.S. 113 (1973).
Roth v. United States, 352 U.S. 964 (1957).
San Antonio Independent School District v. Rodriguez, 411 U.S. 1 (1973).
Shaw v. Reno, 113 S. Ct. 2816 (1993)
Spallone v. United States, 493 U.S. 265 (1990).
Stanford v. Kentucky, 109 S. Ct. 2969 (1989).
Swann v. Charlotte-Mecklenburg Board of Education, 402 U.S. 1 (1971).
Thornburgh v. American College of Obstetricians and Gynecologists, 476 U.S. 747 (1986).
Texas v. Johnson, 491 U.S. 397 (1989).
Trimble v. Gordon, 430 U.S. 762 (1977).
United Auto Workers v. Johnson Controls, Inc., 111 S. Ct. 1196 (1991).
University of California Regents v. Bakke, 438 U.S. 265 (1978).
United States Trust Co. of New York v. New Jersey, 431 U.S. 1 (1977).
United States v. Causby, 328 U.S. 256 (1946).
United States v. Central Eureka Mining Co., 357 U.S. 155 (1958).
United States v. Reese, 92 U.S. (2 Otto) 214 (1876).
United Transportation Union v. Long Island Railroad Co., 455 U.S. 678 (1982).
Wards Cove Packing Co. v. Atonio, 490 U.S. 642 (1990).
Webster v. Reproductive Health Services, 492 U.S. 490 (1989).
Wesberry v. Sanders, 376 U.S. 1 (1964).
West Coast Hotel v. Parrish, 300 U.S. 379 (1937).
Woodson v. North Carolina, 428 U.S. 280 (1976).
Wygant v. Jackson Board of Education, 476 U.S. 267 (1986).
Zorach v. Clauson, 343 U.S. 306 (1952).

Other Federal Cases

Corfield v. Coryell, 6 F. Cas. 546 (C.C.E.D. Pa. 1823).
Roe v. Norton, 522 F.2d 938 (2d Cir. 1975)

State Court Cases

Robins v. Pruneyard Shopping Center, 23 Cal. 3d 899, 592 P.2d 341, 153 Cal. Rptr. 854 (1979).
Campbell v. Morris, 3 H. & Mch. 553 (Md. 1797).
Abbot v. Bayley, 23 Mass. (6 Pick.) 89 (1827).
Roberts v. City of Boston, 59 Mass. (5 Cush.) 198 (1849).
State v. Hunt, 9 So. Car. 1 (1834).
Kamper v. Hawkins, 3 Va. 20 (1790).

SECONDARY SOURCES

Abel, Albert S., "The Commerce Clause in the Constitutional Convention and in Contemporary Comment," *Minnesota Law Review* 25 (1941): 432–99.

Abram, Morris, "Affirmative Action: Fair Shakers and Social Engineers," *Harvard Law Review* 99 (1986): 1312–26.

Ackerman, Bruce A., *Private Property and the Constitution* (New Haven, Conn., 1977).

———, "The Storrs Lectures: Discovering the Constitution," *Yale Law Journal* 93 (1984): 1013–72.

———, *We the People* (Cambridge, Mass., 1991), vol. 1.

Agresto, John, *The Supreme Court and Constitutional Democracy* (Ithaca, N.Y., 1984).

Aleinikoff, T. Alexander, "Updating Statutory Interpretation," *Michigan Law Review* 87 (1988): 20–66.

Alfange, Dean, Jr., "On Judicial Policymaking and Constitutional Change: Another Look at the 'Original Intent' Theory of Constitutional Interpretation," *Hastings Constitutional Law Quarterly* 5 (1978): 603–38.

Amar, Akhil R., "The Bill of Rights as a Constitution," *Yale Law Journal* 100 (1991): 1131–1210.

———, "Philadelphia Revisited: Amending the Constitution outside Article V," *University of Chicago Law Review* 55 (1988): 1043–1104.

Baer, Judith A., *Equality under the Constitution: Reclaiming the Fourteenth Amendment* (Ithaca, N.Y., 1983).

Baker, Liva, *The Justice from Beacon Hill: The Life and Times of Oliver Wendell Holmes* (New York, 1991).

Barber, Soterios A., *On What the Constitution Means* (Baltimore, 1984).

Barnett, Randy E., "Foreword: Judicial Conservatism v. a Principled Judicial Activism," *Harvard Journal of Law and Public Policy* 10 (1987): 273–94.

———, "A Ninth Amendment for Today's Constitution," *Valparaiso University Law Review* 26 (1991): 419–35.

———, "Reconceiving the Ninth Amendment," *Cornell Law Review* 74 (1988): 1–42.

———, "Two Conceptions of the Ninth Amendment," *Harvard Journal of Law and Public Policy* 12 (1989): 29–41.

Barnett, Randy E., ed., *The Rights Retained by the People: The History and Meaning of the Ninth Amendment* (Fairfax, Va., 1989).

Bartholet, Elizabeth, "Application of Title VII to Jobs in High Places," *Harvard Law Review* 95 (1982): 945–1027.

Bassham, Gregory, *Original Intent and the Constitution: A Philosophical Study* (Berkeley, Calif., 1992).

Belz, Herman, *Equality Transformed: A Quarter Century of Affirmative Action* (New Brunswick, N.J., 1991).

———, *A New Birth of Freedom: The Republican Party and Freedmen's Rights, 1861–1866* (Westport, Conn., 1976).

Benedict, Michael Les, *A Compromise of Principle: Congressional Republicans and Reconstruction 1863–1869* (New York, 1974).

———, "Laissez-Faire and Liberty: A Reevaluation of the Origins and Meaning of Laissez-Faire Constitutionalism," *Law and History Review* 3 (1985): 293–322.

Bennett, Robert W., "The Mission of Moral Reasoning in Constitutional Law," *Southern California Law Review* 58 (1985): 647–59.

———, "Objectivity in Constitutional Law," *University of Pennsylvania Law Review* 132 (1984): 445–96.

Berger, Raoul, *Congress v. the Supreme Court* (Cambridge, Mass., 1969).

———, *Government by Judiciary: The Transformation of the Fourteenth Amendment* (Cambridge, Mass., 1977).

———, "The Ninth Amendment," *Cornell Law Review* 61 (1980): 1–26.

Bestor, Albert, "State Sovereignty and Slavery: A Reinterpretation of Proslavery Constitutional Doctrine, 1846–1860," *Journal of the Illinois State Historical Society* 54 (1961): 148.

Bickel, Alexander M., "Foreword: The Passive Virtues," *Harvard Law Review* 75 (1961): 40–79.

———, *The Least Dangerous Branch: The Supreme Court at the Bar of Politics* (Indianapolis, 1962).

———, "The Original Understanding and the Segregation Decision," *Harvard Law Review* 69 (1955): 1–43.

———, *The Supreme Court and the Idea of Progress* (New Haven, Conn., 1970).

Black, Charles L., The People and the Court: Judicial Review in a Democracy (New York, 1960).

———, *Structure and Relationship in Constitutional Law* (Baton Rouge, La., 1969).

Blackstone, Sir William, *Commentaries on the Laws of England*, 4 vols. (London, 1766–1769).

Bobbitt, Philip, *Constitutional Fate: A Theory of the Constitution* (New York, 1982).

———, *Constitutional Interpretation* (Cambridge, Mass., 1991).

Bork, Robert H., "The Constitution, Original Intent, and Economic Rights," *San Diego Law Review* 23 (1986): 823–32.

———, "Neutral Principles and Some First Amendment Problems," *Indiana Law Journal* 47 (1971): 1–35.

———, *The Tempting of America: The Political Seduction of the Law* (New York, 1990).

Brennan, Terry, "Natural Rights and the Constitution: The Original 'Original Intent,'" *Harvard Journal of Law and Public Policy* 15 (1992): 965–1029.

Brest, Paul A., "The Fundamental Rights Controversy: The Essential Contradictions of Normative Constitutional Scholarship," *Yale Law Journal* 90 (1981): 1063–1109.

———, "The Misconceived Quest for the Original Understanding," *Boston University Law Review* 60 (1980): 204–54.

———, "The Substance of Process," *Ohio State Law Journal* 42 (1981): 131–42.

———, "Who Decides," *Southern California Law Review* 58 (1985): 661–71.

Brock, William R., *An American Crisis: Congress and Reconstruction 1865–1867* (New York, 1963).

Buchanan, G. Sidney, *The Quest for Freedom: A Legal History of the Thirteenth Amendment* (Houston, 1976).

Burt, Robert A., "The Constitution of the Family," in *Supreme Court Review: 1979*, ed. Philip B. Kurland and Gerhard Casper (Chicago, 1980).

Calhoun, John C., "Fort Hill Address," in *Papers of John C. Calhoun*, ed. Clyde N. Wilson, 18 vols. (Columbia, S.C., 1959–1988), 11:413–40.

Caplan, Russell L., "The History and Meaning of the Ninth Amendment," *Virginia Law Review* 69 (1983): 223–68.

Chang, David, "Conflict, Coherence, and Constitutional Intent," *Iowa Law Review* 72 (1987): 753–890.

———, "Discriminatory Impact, Affirmative Action, and Innocent Victims: Judicial Conservatism or Conservative Justices," *Columbia Law Review* 91 (1991): 790–844.

Chemerinsky, Erwin, "Foreword: The Vanishing Constitution," *Harvard Law Review* 103 (1989): 43–104.

Choper, Jesse H., "Consequences of Supreme Court Decisions Upholding Constitutional Rights," *Michigan Law Review* 83 (1984): 1–212.

———, *Judicial Review and the National Political Process* (Chicago, 1980).

Clinton, Robert L., *Marbury v. Madison and Judicial Review* (Lawrence, Kans., 1989).

Conkle, Daniel O., "The Second Death of Substantive Due Process," *Indiana Law Journal* 62 (1987): 215–22.

Cooley, Thomas M., *A Treatise on the Constitutional Limitations Which Rest upon the Legislative Power* (Boston, 1868; repr. New York, 1972).

Corwin, Edward S., "The Doctrine of Due Process of Law before the Civil War," *Harvard Law Review* 24 (1911): 366–479.

———, *The Doctrine of Judicial Review* (Princeton, N.J., 1914).

Cox, LaWanda, and John H. Cox, "Negro Suffrage and Republican Politics: The Problem of Motivation in Reconstruction Historiography," *Journal of Southern History* 33 (1967) 303–30.

———, *Politics, Principle, and Prejudice 1865–1866* (London, 1963).

Crosskey, William W., *Politics and the Constitution in the History of the United States*, 2 vols. (Chicago, 1953).

Curtis, Michael Kent, *No State Shall Abridge: The Fourteenth Amendment and the Bill of Rights* (Durham, N.C., 1986).

D'Souza, Dinesh, *Illiberal Education: The Politics of Race and Sex on Campus* (New York, 1991).

Dahl, Robert A., "Decision-Maker in a Democracy: The Supreme Court as a National Policy-Maker," *Journal of Public Law* 6 (1957): 279–95.

Delgado, Richard, "The Ethereal Scholar: Does Critical Legal Studies Have What Minorities Want?" *Harvard Civil Rights–Civil Liberties Law Review* 22 (1987): 311–22.

Dworkin, Ronald M., "The Forum of Principle," *New York University Law Review* 56 (1981): 469–518.

———, "Law as Interpretation," *Texas Law Review* 60 (1982): 527–50.

———, *Law's Empire* (Cambridge, Mass., 1986).

———, *A Matter of Principle* (Cambridge, Mass., 1985).

———, *Taking Rights Seriously* (Cambridge, Mass., 1977).

———, "Unenumerated Rights: Whether and How *Roe* Should Be Overruled," *University of Chicago Law Review* 59 (1992): 381–432.

Easterbrook, Frank H., "Legal Interpretation and the Power of the Judiciary," *Harvard Journal of Law and Public Policy* 7 (1981): 87–99.

Ely, John Hart, *Democracy and Distrust: A Theory of Judicial Review* (Cambridge, Mass., 1980).

———, "The Wages of Crying Wolf: A Comment on *Roe v. Wade*," *Yale Law Journal* 82 (1973): 920–49.

Epstein, Richard A., *Takings: Private Property and the Power of Eminent Domain* (Chicago, 1985).

————, "Toward a Revitalization of the Contracts Clause," *University of Chicago Law Review* 51 (1984): 703-52.

Eskridge, William N., "Dynamic Statutory Interpretation," *University of Pennsylvania Law Review* 135 (1987): 1479-1556.

————, "Gadamer/Statutory Interpretation," *Columbia Law Review* 90 (1990): 609-81.

————, "Overruling Supreme Court Statutory Interpretation Decisions," *Yale Law Journal* 101 (1991): 331-455.

Fairman, Charles, *Reconstruction and Reunion*, pt. 1 (New York, 1972).

Fallon, Richard H., Jr., "A Constructivist-Coherence Theory of Constitutional Interpretation," *Harvard Law Review* 100 (1987): 1189-1287.

————, "What Is Republicanism, and Is It Worth Reviving," *Harvard Law Review* 102 (1989): 1695-1735.

Farrand, Max, ed., *The Records of the Federal Convention*, 4 vols., rev. ed. (New Haven, Conn., 1937).

Fehrenbacher, Don E., *The Dred Scott Case: Its Significance in American Law and Politics* (New York, 1978).

Finkelman, Paul, *An Imperfect Union: Slavery, Comity, and Federalism* (Chapel Hill, N.C., 1981).

————, "Prelude to the Fourteenth Amendment: Black Legal Rights in the Antebellum North," *Rutgers Law Journal* 17 (1986): 415-82.

Fiss, Owen M., "Foreword: The Forms of Justice," *Harvard Law Review* 93 (1979): 1-58.

Foner, Eric, *Free Soil, Free Labor, Free Men* (New York, 1970).

————, *Reconstruction: America's Unfinished Revolution 1863-1877* (New York, 1988).

Freedman, Ann E., "Sex Equality, Sex Differences, and the Supreme Court," *Yale Law Journal* 92 (1984): 913-69.

Freehling, William W., *Prelude to Civil War: The Nullification Crisis in South Carolina* (New York, 1966).

Gillette, William, *The Right to Vote: Politics and the Passage of the Fifteenth Amendment* (Baltimore, 1965).

Glendon, Mary Ann, *Abortion and Divorce in Western Law* (Cambridge, Mass., 1987).

————, *Rights Talk: The Impoverishment of Political Discourse* (New York, 1991).

Goldstein, Anne E., "History, Homosexuality, and Political Values: Searching for the Hidden Determinant of *Bowers v. Hardwick*," *Yale Law Journal* 97 (1988): 1073-1104.

Graglia, Lino A., "Constitutional Theory: The Attempted Justification for the Supreme Court's Liberal Program," *Texas Law Review* 65 (1987): 789-98.

————, *Disaster by Decree: The Supreme Court Decisions on Race and the Schools* (Ithaca, N.Y., 1976).

————, "Judicial Activism: Even on the Right, It's Wrong," *Public Interest* 95 (1989): 57-74.

Graham, Howard J., *Everyman's Constitution* (Madison, Wis., 1968).

Greenawalt, R. Kent, "The Enduring Significance of Neutral Principles," *Columbia Law Review* 78 (1978): 982-1021.

Grey, Thomas C., "The Constitution as Scripture," *Stanford Law Review* 37 (1984): 1-25.

————, "Do We Have an Unwritten Constitution?" *Stanford Law Review* 27 (1975): 703-18.

————, "Origins of the Unwritten Constitution: Fundamental Law in American Revolutionary Thought," *Stanford Law Review* 30 (1978): 843–94.

Haines, Charles G., *The American Doctrine of Judicial Supremacy* (1932; repr. New York, 1973).

Hamburger, Philip A., "Natural Rights, Natural Law, and American Constitutions," *Yale Law Journal* 102 (1993): 907–60.

Hamilton, Alexander, John Jay, and James Madison, *The Federalist Papers*, ed. Jacob E. Cooke (Middletown, Conn., 1961).

Hart, Henry M., Jr., "Professor Crosskey and Judicial Review," *Harvard Law Review* 67 (1954): 1456–86.

Heins, Marjorie, "Banning Words: A Comment on 'Words That Wound,' " *Harvard Civil Rights-Civil Liberties Law Review* 18 (1983): 585–624.

Henkin, Louis, "Is There a 'Political Question' Doctrine?" *Yale Law Journal* 85 (1976): 597–625.

Heymann, Philip B., and Douglas E. Barzelay, "The Forest and the Trees: *Roe v. Wade* and Its Critics," *Boston University Law Review* 53 (1973): 765–84.

Howe, Lowell J., "The Meaning of 'Due Process of Law' prior to the Adoption of the Fourteenth Amendment," *California Law Review* 18 (1930): 583–610.

Hutson, James H., "The Bill of Rights and the American Revolutionary Experience," in *A Culture of Rights: The Bill of Rights in Philosophy, Politics, and Law—1791 and 1991*, ed. Michael J. Lacey and Knud Haakonssen, pp. 62–97 (New York, 1991).

————, "The Creation of the Constitution: The Integrity of the Documentary Record," *Texas Law Review* 65 (1986): 1–39.

Hyman, Harold M., *A More Perfect Union: The Impact of the Civil War and Reconstruction on the Constitution* (New York, 1973).

Hyman, Harold M., and William M. Wiecek, *Equal Justice under Law: Constitutional Development 1835–1875* (New York, 1982).

Jaffa, Harry, "What Were the 'Original Intentions' of the Framers of the Constitution of the United States?" *University of Puget Sound Law Review* 10 (1987): 343–448.

James, Joseph B., *The Framing of the Fourteenth Amendment* (Urbana, Ill., 1956).

Johannsen, Robert W., ed., *The Lincoln-Douglas Debates of 1858* (New York, 1965).

Kaczorowski, Robert J., *The Politics of Judicial Interpretation: The Federal Courts, Department of Justice, and Civil Rights, 1866–1876* (New York, 1985).

————, "Revolutionary Constitutionalism in the Era of the Civil War and Reconstruction," *New York University Law Review* 61 (1986): 863–940.

Kaden, Lewis B., "Politics, Money, and State Sovereignty: The Judicial Role," *Columbia Law Review* 79 (1979): 847–97.

Kahn, Ali, "The Invasion of Sexual Privacy," *San Diego Law Review* 23 (1986): 957–78.

Kay, Richard S., "Adherence to the Original Intentions in Constitutional Adjudication: Three Objections and Responses," *Northwestern University Law Review* 82 (1988): 228–92.

————, "The Illegality of the Constitution," *Constitutional Commentary* 4 (1987): 57–80.

Kelly, Alfred H., "Clio and the Court: An Illicit Love Affair," in *Supreme Court Review: 1965*, ed. Philip B. Kurland (Chicago, 1965).

Kendrick, Benjamin B., *The Journal of the Joint Committee on Reconstruction, 39th Congress, 1865–67* (New York, 1914).

Kent, James, *Commentaries on American Law*, 10th ed., 4 vols. (Boston, 1860).

Kerber, Linda K., "Making Republicanism Useful," *Yale Law Journal* 97 (1988): 1663–72.

Kettner, James H., *The Development of American Citizenship, 1608–1870* (Chapel Hill, N.C., 1978).

Kohl, Robert, "The Civil Rights Act of 1866: Its Hour Come Round at Last: *Jones v. Albert Mayer Co.*," *Virginia Law Review* 55 (1969): 272–300.

Kurland, Philip B., and Ralph Lerner, eds., *The Founders Constitution*, 5 vols. (Chicago, 1987).

Law, Sylvia A., "Homosexuality and the Social Meaning of Gender," *Wisconsin Law Review* (1988): 187–236.

———, "Rethinking Sex and the Constitution," *University of Pennsylvania Law Review* 132 (1984): 955–1040.

Lawrence, Charles R., "If He Hollers Let Him Go: Regulating Racist Speech on Campus," *Duke Law Journal* (1990): 431–83.

Levinson, Sanford, *Constitutional Faith* (Princeton, N.J., 1988).

Levy, Leonard W., *The Law of the Commonwealth and Chief Justice Shaw* (Cambridge, Mass., 1957).

———, *Original Intent and the Framers' Constitution* (New York, 1988).

Leyh, Gregory, ed., *Legal Hermeneutics: History, Theory, and Practice* (Chicago, 1992).

Lieber, Francis, *The Miscellaneous Writings of Francis Lieber* (Philadelphia, 1880).

Littleton, Christine A., "Reconstructing Sexual Equality," *California Law Review* 75 (1987): 1279–1337.

Lofgren, Charles A., "The Original Understanding of Original Intent," *Constitutional Commentary* 5 (1988): 77–113.

———, "The Origins of the Tenth Amendment," in *"Government from Reflection and Choice": Constitutional Essays on War, Foreign Relations, and Federalism*, by Charles A. Lofgren, pp. 70–115 (New York, 1986).

Lupu, Ira C., "Untangling the Strands of the Fourteenth Amendment," *Michigan Law Review* 77 (1979): 981–1077.

McAffee, Thomas B., "The Bill of Rights, Social Contract Theory, and the Rights 'Retained' by the People," *Southern University Law Review* 16 (1992): 267–305.

———, "The Original Meaning of the Ninth Amendment," *Columbia Law Review* 90 (1990): 1215–1320.

———, "Prolegomena to a Meaningful Debate of the 'Unwritten Constitution' Thesis," *University of Cincinnati Law Review* 61 (1992): 107–70.

McDonald, Forrest, *Novus Ordo Seclorum: The Intellectual Origins of the Constitution* (Lawrence, Kans., 1985).

McDowell, Gary L., *The Constitution and Contemporary Constitutional Theory* (Cumberland, Va., 1985).

Macedo, Stephen, "Majority Power, Moral Skepticism, and the New Right's Constitution," in *Economic Liberties and the Judiciary*, ed. James A. Dorn and Henry G. Manne, pp. 111–37 (Fairfax, Va., 1987).

———, *The New Right v. the Constitution* (Washington, D.C., 1987).

McKitrick, Eric, *Andrew Johnson and Reconstruction* (Chicago, 1960).

McLaughlin, Andrew C., *A Constitutional History of the United States* (New York, 1935).

McPherson, James M., *The Struggle for Equality: The Abolitionists and the Negro in the Civil War and Reconstruction* (Princeton, N.J., 1964).

Maltz, Earl M., "The Appeal of Originalism," *Utah Law Review* (1987): 773–805.

————, *Civil Rights, the Constitution, and Congress, 1863–1869* (Lawrence, Kans., 1990).

————, "The Concept of Equal Protection of the Laws—A Historical Inquiry," *San Diego Law Review* 22 (1985): 499–540.

————, "The Failure of Attacks on Constitutional Originalism," *Constitutional Commentary* 4 (1987): 43–56.

————, "Fourteenth Amendment Concepts in the Antebellum Era," *American Journal of Legal History* 32 (1988): 305–46.

————, "Portrait of a Man in the Middle—Mr. Justice Powell, Equal Protection, and the Pure Classification Problem," *Ohio State Law Journal* 42 (1979): 941–64.

————, "The Prospects for a Revival of Conservative Activism in Constitutional Jurisprudence," *Georgia Law Review* 24 (1990): 629–68.

————, " 'Separate but Equal' and the Law of Common Carriers in the Era of the Fourteenth Amendment," *Rutgers Law Journal* 17 (1986): 553–68.

————, "Some New Thoughts on an Old Problem: The Role of the Intent of the Framers in Constitutional Theory," *Boston University Law Review* 63 (1983): 811–51.

————, "Statutory Interpretation and Legislative Power: The Case for a Modified Intentionalist Approach," *Tulane Law Review* 63 (1988): 1–28.

————, "The Supreme Court and the Quality of Political Dialogue," *Constitutional Commentary* 5 (1988): 375–91.

————, "Unenumerated Rights and Originalist Methodology: A Comment on the Ninth Amendment Symposium," *Chicago-Kent Law Review* 64 (1988): 981–85.

Matsuda, Mari J., "Accent, Antidiscrimination Law, and a Jurisprudence for the Last Reconstruction," *Yale Law Journal* 100 (1991): 1329–1407.

————, "Public Response to Racist Speech: Considering the Victim's Story," *Michigan Law Review* 87 (1989): 2320–81.

Meese, Edwin, "Address of Edwin Meese III . . . before the American Bar Association, July 9, 1985," in *The Great Debate: Interpreting Our Written Constitution*, ed. Federalist Society for Law and Public Policy (Washington, D.C., 1986).

Michael, Helen K., "The Role of Natural Law in Early American Constitutionalism: Did the Founders Contemplate Judicial Enforcement of 'Unwritten' Constitutional Rights?" *North Carolina Law Review* 69 (1991): 421–90.

Michelman, Frank I., "Law's Republic," *Yale Law Journal* 97 (1988): 1493–1538.

————, "Saving Old Glory: On Constitutional Iconography," *Stanford Law Review* 42 (1990): 1337–64.

————, "The Supreme Court, 1985 Term—Foreword: Traces of Self-Government," *Harvard Law Review* 100 (1986): 4–77.

Miller, Arthur S., *Toward Increased Judicial Activism* (Westport, Conn., 1982).

Miller, Charles, *The Supreme Court and the Uses of History* (Cambridge, Mass., 1969).

Mitchell, Lawrence E., "The Ninth Amendment and the Jurisprudence of Original Intention," *Georgetown Law Journal* 74 (1986): 1719–42.

Monaghan, Henry P., "Our Perfect Constitution," *New York University Law Review* 56 (1981): 353–96.

Mott, Rodney L., *Due Process of Law: A Historical and Analytical Treatise of the Principles and Methods Followed by the Courts in the Application of the Concept of the "Law of the Land"* (Indianapolis, 1926).

Munzer, Stephen R., and James W. Nickel, "Does the Constitution Mean What It Always Meant?" *Columbia Law Review* 77 (1977): 1029–62.

Murphy, Paul L., *The Constitution in Crisis Times, 1918–1969* (New York, 1972).

Nagel, Robert F., *Constitutional Cultures: The Mentality and Culture of Judicial Review* (Berkeley, Calif., 1989).

————, "Rationalism in Constitutional Law," *Constitutional Commentary* 4 (1987): 9–24.

Nedelsky, Jennifer, *Private Property and the Limits of American Constitutionalism: The Madisonian Framework and Its Legacy* (Chicago, 1990).

Nelson, William E., *The Fourteenth Amendment: From Political Principle to Judicial Doctrine* (Cambridge, Mass., 1988).

Nowak, John E., Ronald D. Rotunda, and Nelson Young, *Constitutional Law*, 2d ed. (St. Paul, Minn., 1982).

Pangle, Thomas L., "Comments on Cass Sunstein's 'Republicanism and the Preference Problem,'" *Chicago-Kent Law Review* 66 (1990): 205–12.

Parker, Richard A., "The Past of Constitutional Theory—and Its Future," *Ohio State Law Journal* 42 (1981): 223–60.

Patterson, Bennett, *The Forgotten Ninth Amendment* (Indianapolis, 1955).

Pearson, Albert M., and Paul M. Kurtz, "The Abortion Controversy: A Study in Law and Politics," *Harvard Journal of Law and Public Policy* 8 (1985): 427–64.

Perry, Michael J., "Abortion, the Public Morals, and the Police Power: The Ethical Function of Substantive Due Process," *U.C.L.A. Law Review* 23 (1976): 689–736.

————, *The Constitution, the Courts, and Human Rights* (New Haven, Conn., 1982).

————, *Love and Power: The Role of Religion and Morality in American Politics* (New York, 1991).

Posner, Richard, "Law and Literature: A Puzzle Reargued," *Virginia Law Review* 72 (1986): 1351–92.

————, "Legal Formalism, Legal Realism, and the Interpretation of Statutes and the Constitution," *Case Western Law Review* 37 (1986–1987): 179–217.

Powell, H. Jefferson, "The Original Understanding of Original Intent," *Harvard Law Review* 98 (1985): 885–948.

————, "Parchment Matters: A Meditation on the Constitution," *Iowa Law Review* 71 (1986): 1427–35.

————, "Rules for Originalists," *Virginia Law Review* 73 (1987): 659–99.

Redlich, Norman, "Are There Certain Rights . . . Retained by the People?" *New York University Law Review* 37 (1961): 787–808.

Rehnquist, William H., "The Notion of a Living Constitution," *Texas Law Review* 54 (1976): 693–706.

Richards, David A. J., "Constitutional Legitimacy and Constitutional Privacy," *New York University Law Review* 61 (1986): 800–862.

————, *Foundations of American Constitutionalism* (New York, 1989).

————, *Toleration and the Constitution* (New York, 1986).

Rosberg, Gerald, "Aliens and Equal Protection: Why Not the Right to Vote?" *Michigan Law Review* 75 (1977): 1092–1136.

Rosenfeld, Michel, "Decoding Richmond: Affirmative Action and the Elusive Meaning of Constitutional Equality," *Michigan Law Review* 87 (1989): 1729–94.

Rotunda, Ronald D., "The Doctrine of Constitutional Preemption and Other Limitations on Tenth Amendment Restrictions," *University of Pennsylvania Law Review* 132 (1984): 289–326.

Rubenfeld, Jeb, "The Right of Privacy," *Harvard Law Review* 102 (1989): 737–807.

Ruthergelen, George A., "Title VII Class Actions," *University of Chicago Law Review* 47 (1980): 688–742.

Sadurski, Wojiech, "Conventional Morality and Judicial Standards," *Virginia Law Review* 73 (1987): 339–98.

Sager, Laurence G., "Rights Skepticism and Process-based Responses," *New York University Law Review* 56 (1981): 417–45.

———, "You Can Raise the First, Hide behind the Fourth, and Plead the Fifth, But What on Earth Can You Do with the Ninth Amendment?" *Chicago-Kent Law Review* 64 (1988): 239–64.

Scalia, Antonin, "Originalism: The Lesser Evil," *University of Cincinnati Law Review* 57 (1989): 849–65.

Schlag, Pierre, "Framers' Intent: The Illegitimate Uses of History," *University of Puget Sound Law Review* 8 (1985): 285–330.

Schwartz, Bernard, ed., *The Bill of Rights: A Documentary History*, 2 vols. (New York, 1971).

———, *Swann's Way: The School Busing Case and the Supreme Court* (New York, 1971).

Sedler, Robert, "The Legitimacy Debate in Constitutional Theory: An Assessment and a Different Perspective," *Ohio State Law Journal* 44 (1983): 93–137.

Sherry, Suzanna, "The Founders' Unwritten Constitution," *University of Chicago Law Review* 54 (1987): 1127–77.

———, "The Ghost of Liberalism Past," *Harvard Law Review* 105 (1991): 918–34.

———, "Natural Law in the States," *University of Cincinnati Law Review* 61 (1992): 171–222.

———, "The Ninth Amendment: Righting an Unwritten Constitution," *Chicago-Kent Law Review* 64 (1988): 1001–14.

Siegan, Bernard H., *Economic Liberties and the Constitution* (Chicago, 1980).

Simon, Larry G., "The Authority of the Framers of the Constitution: Can Originalist Interpretation Be Justified?" *California Law Review* 73 (1985): 1482–1539.

Spann, Girardeau A., *Race against the Court: The Supreme Court and Minorities in Contemporary America* (New York, 1993).

Stewart, Richard B., "Problems of Federalism in National Environmental Policy," *Yale Law Journal* 86 (1977): 1196–1272.

Stoddard, Thomas B., "*Bowers v. Hardwick*: Precedent by Predilection," *University of Chicago Law Review* 54 (1987): 648–56.

Stone, Geoffrey R., "Flag Burning and the Constitution," *Iowa Law Review* (1989): 111–24.

Storing, Herbert J., ed., *The Complete Anti-Federalist*, 7 vols. (Chicago, 1981).

Story, Joseph, *Commentaries on the Constitution of the United States*, 3 vols. (Boston, 1833).

Strauss, David A., "Afterword: The Role of a Bill of Rights," *University of Chicago Law Review* 59 (1992): 539–66.

Strossen, Nadine, "Regulating Racist Speech on Campus: A Modest Proposal," *Duke Law Journal* (1990): 484–573.

Sullivan, Kathleen M., "Sins of Discrimination: Last Term's Affirmative Action Cases," *Harvard Law Review* 100 (1986): 78–99.

Sunstein, Cass R., "Beyond the Republican Revival," *Yale Law Journal* 97 (1988): 1539–90.

———, "Interest Groups in American Public Law," *Stanford Law Review* 38 (1985): 29–87.

———, "Neutrality in Constitutional Law (with Special Reference to Pornography, Abortion, and Surrogacy)," *Columbia Law Review* 92 (1992): 1–52.

"The Supreme Court—1985 Term," *Harvard Law Review* 100 (1986): 100–305.

"A Survey of the Present Statutory and Case Law on Abortion: The Contradictions and Problems," *University of Illinois Law Forum* (1972): 177–98.

Suthon, Walter J., Jr., "The Dubious Origin of the Fourteenth Amendment," *Tulane Law Review* 28 (1953): 22–44.

"Symposium: "The Jurisprudence of Takings," *Columbia Law Review* 88 (1988): 1581–1795.

"Symposium: The Republican Civic Tradition," *Yale Law Journal* 97 (1988): 1493–1724.

tenBroek, Jacobus, *The Antislavery Origins of the Fourteenth Amendment* (Berkeley, Calif., 1951).

Tiedman, Christopher G., *A Treatise on the Limitations of Police Power in the United States* (1886; repr. New York, 1971).

Tribe, Laurence H., *American Constitutional Law*, 2d ed. (Mineola, N.Y., 1988).

———, *Constitutional Choices* (Cambridge, Mass., 1985).

———, "In What Vision of the Constitution Must the Law Be Color-Blind?" *John Marshall Law Review* 20 (1986): 201–8.

Tribe, Laurence H., and Michael C. Dorf, *On Reading the Constitution* (Cambridge, Mass., 1991).

Tucker, St. George, *Blackstone's Commentaries. With Notes of Reference to the Constitution and Laws of the Federal Government of the United States and of the Commonwealth of Virginia*, 5 vols. (Philadelphia, 1803).

Tushnet, Mark V., "The Dilemmas of Liberal Constitutionalism," *Ohio State Law Journal* 42 (1981): 411–26.

———, "Following the Rules Laid Down: A Critique of Interpretivism and Neutral Principles," *Harvard Law Review* 96 (1983): 781–827.

Van Alstyne, William, "The Fourteenth Amendment, The 'Right' to Vote, and the Understanding of the Thirty-Ninth Congress," in *Supreme Court Review: 1965*, ed. Philip B. Kurland (Chicago, 1965).

Viera, Norman, "*Hardwick* and the Right of Privacy," *University of Chicago Law Review* 55 (1988): 1181–92.

Warren, Charles, *Congress, the Constitution, and the Supreme Court* (Boston, 1925).

———, *The Supreme Court in United States History*, 3 vols. (Boston, 1922).

Wechsler, Herbert, "The Courts and the Constitution," *Columbia Law Review* 65 (1965): 1001–14.

———, "The Political Safeguards of Federalism: The Role of the States in the Composition and Selection of the National Government," *Columbia Law Review* 54 (1954): 543–60.

———, "Toward Neutral Principles of Constitutional Law," *Harvard Law Review* 73 (1959): 1–35.

Weisberg, Robert H., "Text into Theory: A Literary Approach to the Constitution," *Georgia Law Review* 20 (1986): 939–94.

Wellington, Harry H., "Common Law Rules and Constitutional Double Standards," *Yale Law Journal* 83 (1973): 223–312.

West, Robin, "Equality Theory, Marital Rape, and the Promise of the Fourteenth Amendment," *Florida Law Review* 42 (1990): 45–79.

Wofford, John G., "The Blinding Light: The Uses of History in Constitutional Interpretation," *University of Chicago Law Review* 31 (1964): 502–33.

Wolfe, Christopher, *The Rise of Modern Judicial Review: From Constitutional Interpretation to Judge-made Law* (New York, 1986).

Wood, Gordon S., *The Creation of the American Republic, 1776-1787* (New York, 1969).

Wright, J. Skelly, "Professor Bickel, the Scholarly Tradition, and the Supreme Court," *Harvard Law Review* 84 (1971): 769-805.

Zuckert, Michael P., "Completing the Constitution: The Thirteenth Amendment," *Constitutional Commentary* 4 (1987): 259-83.

———, "Congressional Power under the Fourteenth Amendment—The Original Understanding of Section Five," *Constitutional Commentary* 3 (1986): 123-56.

INDEX